Kieran
READ

Kieran READ

TRIBUTE TO A GREAT EIGHT

Matt Elliott

Bateman

This book is dedicated to the sons
of my dear friends, Kevin and Robyn —
Finley, Toby and Leo.

Text © Matt Elliott, 2015
Design and typography © David Bateman Ltd, 2015

Published in 2015 by David Bateman Ltd
30 Tarndale Grove, Albany, Auckland, New Zealand

www.batemanpublishing.co.nz

A catalogue record for this book is available from the
National Library of New Zealand.

ISBN 978-1-86953-918-4

Publisher: Bill Honeybone
Book design: Cheryl Smith, Macarn Design
Printed in China by Asia Pacific Offset Ltd

Contents

Introduction

16 November 2013
Twickenham, London

The All Blacks are on their annual end-of-year tour to the northern hemisphere, facing England at 'the home of rugby'. They are on the verge of becoming the first team in the professional era (that is, since 1996) to go through a year unbeaten. They've won all 11 games played, and two more victories will see them achieve the feat.

But that accomplishment is far in the back of their minds as they take the field on a cool, grey London afternoon. They are only thinking about one game they have to win, only one team to beat — England. They're not up against just the English squad of 23 players, but also a crowd of 80,000 English supporters. A sprinkling of expectant All Blacks fans are in among them. Just like the players wearing the rose on their jerseys, the crowd is loud and vociferous. For them, there is no greater victory than one over the All Blacks. Their team could lose every other game they play in an international season, but if they beat the All Blacks, the year will be considered a success. Although the English have only beaten the All Blacks five times and drawn once in London since 1905, the men wearing the silver fern know how much the English players, fans and media delight in their losses.

They experienced it 12 months earlier when a rampant England team sent the All Blacks into summer with a crushing 38–21 loss. The All Blacks never want to lose a game, and they especially don't want to lose a game to England, in England!

After the anthems and the English crowd responding to the haka with resounding choruses of 'Swing Low, Sweet Chariot', play begins.

The All Blacks know that if they can dampen the crowd's enthusiasm early in the game by getting points on the board, the less-charged atmosphere will take some of the fire out of the English players. So the All Blacks swing into attack from the kick-off and, within two minutes of play, find themselves with the lineout throw five metres from the English line, on the left-hand side of the field.

Keven Mealamu throws to the lineout, but it is a scrappy one and the aggressive, disruptive English defence drives the All Blacks back several metres. Liam Messam secures the ball but is quickly upended by an English defender. All Black forwards are at the ruck quickly to shield the ball.

Halfback Aaron Smith, aware of the speed with which the English backs will rush up to defend against his teammates on his right, opts to pass left to a narrow, congested blindside where Richie McCaw, Dan Carter, Kieran Read and Julian Savea are waiting. McCaw passes to Carter in one movement. Carter just manages to get his pass away before falling to the ground in a tackle. But the ball bounces before it gets to Read, giving the English defence a fraction of a second more time to move up on the big number eight. Scooping up the ball as the English winger Ashton wraps his arms around him, Read deliberately runs a diagonal line towards the corner flag. The touchline is a mere four steps away. The white line, an assistant referee and even the crowd seated at ground level are looming up fast. Two other English players, his opposite Vunipola and halfback Dickson, smother Read, driving him towards touch. Such is the power in Read's legs, he is able to hold himself up and slow the English drive. Just before crossing the touchline, holding the ball in his right hand, he hooks a pass around behind him and infield to where Savea is waiting. The big winger snaps onto the pass and strides unimpeded to the try line.

That split-second of brilliance from Read exhibits his power, his subtlety, his awareness of the situation and the position of his teammates, as well as the All Blacks' refusal to surrender the ball and to keep striving for scoring opportunities.

Two weeks later, Read is crowned World Rugby Player of the Year, capping a stellar season for the only All Black to have come from Papakura's Rosehill College.

The Boy from Papakura

Kieran James Read was born in Papakura, south of Auckland in the Counties-Manukau region, on 26 October 1985, one of three sons to Terry and Marilyn. He attended Opaheke Primary School, where Marilyn has taught for many years, and initially played junior rugby for the Drury Rugby Club. He then progressed to Rosehill Intermediate, switched to the Papakura Rugby Club, and played in the Counties-Manukau Roller Mills side. Like so many parents, Terry and Marilyn would drive the young Kieran to his games and reward him with some sort of treat after matches. Being chosen for a Counties-Manukau age-group team saw Kieran receive his first All Blacks jersey, albeit a replica, but the sort so many boys wear with pride, playing schoolyard games where they imagine themselves scoring winning tries or kicking winning goals for the All Blacks. Another schoolyard activity Read was a keen participant in was wrestling, based on the very popular World Wrestling Federation shows on television at the time.

When Counties was part of the Blues catchment, the Reads would travel up to Eden Park to watch Super Rugby matches, and the first time Read attended a test match was at that ground.

Read's move to secondary school in 1999 was a short-distance one, as Rosehill College stands right next to the intermediate school. He played rugby in winter and cricket in summer and it was his potential in both codes that saw him offered a sports scholarship in 2000 to the prestigious Saint Kentigern College in Pakuranga. But while being at Saint Kentigern meant the prospect of playing top-flight college First XV rugby and First XI cricket, the fourth-form Read wasn't comfortable in his new surroundings. He later told *Press* reporter Richard Knowler:

> '*I suppose coming from where I did, I had always been at a co-ed school and had kind of never been to a school that was so formal, and that type of thing. It just wasn't me and I wasn't enjoying it as much as what I had at Rosehill. I just wanted to be among my mates.*'

So with his parents' blessing, Read returned to his mates and the modest Rosehill College. Their First XV, which he played in for three years, 'was great fun … we weren't the greatest team around but we showed up and enjoyed each other's company'. They didn't even get to play against the top team in the Counties competition, Wesley's First XV. Wesley had produced a number of All Blacks, the best-known of whom was Jonah Lomu, who was the young Read's favourite player. Games against that college, albeit their Second XV, were the pinnacle of the season and wins were savoured by Read and his teammates in the blue-and-red jerseys of Rosehill.

While Read may refer to his college rugby days as 'fun', it wasn't just about fun for the lean boy with a big head of hair who by the fifth form had shot up to over six feet tall.

James Fraser, who coached the young Read, reminisced to Richard Knowler:

> 'I suppose you could say he was fearless. If you looked at him back then, there wasn't much to him — he was pretty lanky. He wasn't the type to get into fights. You can play some pretty rough teams at times around here … but he was more the type to tell the hot-headed guys to pull their heads in.'

Read has always been quick to credit Fraser with helping him establish a training regime, as well as goal-setting. The two often started cold winter mornings, when most other teenagers are struggling to get out of bed, with committed one-on-one training sessions. 'He put a pretty big emphasis on me and got me coming in and doing some extra training in the mornings, and talking to different guys about the mental stuff and nutrition,' recalled Read. 'He invested a little bit into me, actually, and that probably set up some professionalism in me and showed me what I could get out of the game.' Read's application to all aspects of school life saw him become part of the student leaders' group in 2002, and he was appointed Head Boy in 2003, and was the recipient of Sportsman of the Year and Sports All Rounder prizes as captain of the First XI cricket team and vice-captain of the First XV rugby team.

Despite the low profile of the Rosehill senior rugby team, Read, modelling himself on Richie McCaw, renowned for his turnover skills and tireless tackling, was selected for regional age-group rugby sides. But it was when he was wearing cricket whites, inspired by national heroes such as Martin Crowe and Stephen Fleming, that he was seen by many as an international star in the making.

Read (who now claims to be a bit embarrassed by mentions of his cricketing days) was selected as an opening batsman to play for the Northern Districts Under 17 cricket team for the annual national age-group tournament, which was held in Napier in January of 2002. His teammates included future test cricketers Daniel Flynn and BJ Watling, and one-day international batsman Anton Devcich.

After the week-long tournament — a mix of one-day and two-day matches — Central Districts was crowned champions while Read's Northern Districts had three draws, a win and a loss. Their win, by 11 runs, came over Canterbury with Read leading the way with an accomplished 86, the third-highest score of the tournament. He also scored another well-composed half-century in the loss to Wellington. His total of 181 tournament runs at an average of 60.33 saw him named in the 'Team of the Tournament', along with Doug Winger, Derek de Boorder, Sam McKay, Chris McDowell (Auckland), Todd Astle, Byron Newton (Canterbury), Daniel Bolstad, Daniel MacDonald (Central Districts), Craig Smith (Otago), Michael Martin, and Chris Spring (Wellington). While several in that selection progressed to play first-class cricket, and Todd Astle later played one test for New Zealand, few could have foreseen what international honours lay ahead for Read.

At the start of the next cricket season later that year, he was chosen to play for Counties-Manukau in the annual Fergus Hickey Rosebowl district tournament. Read found himself in the company of not only school-age players but grown men, and batted at either number three or five. While adept and patient when it came to occupying time at the crease, he did not find scoring runs easy and, apart from a 38 against Poverty Bay, had a run of scores of less than 10.

In January of 2003, Read returned to Napier with the Under 17 side for the annual tournament. This time, his Northern Districts side won the title. He batted three times (including lining up against an Auckland team that had one Martin Guptill in its ranks), almost replicating his efforts of the previous tournament, scoring a total of 174 runs at an average of 58.66. He again enjoyed the Canterbury bowling, scoring 74 against them, and, once again, was named in the tournament team. Joining him were Derek de Boorder, Marc Ellison, Carl Frauenstein (Auckland), Anton Devcich, Sam McLeod, Tarron Te Moni (Northern Districts), Kevin Forde, Hamish Templeton (Wellington), Chris Small, Brent Findlay (Canterbury) and Kieran Noema-Barnett (Otago).

'All through school I was the captain of Counties and Northern Districts age-group cricket teams,' he told rugby writer Toby Robson. 'So that was probably my only brush with leadership. I enjoyed doing it from the technical side more than anything else, but I didn't feel like I was a leader.'

Come the winter months and Read (weighing a sprightly 92 kg) was chosen as an open-side flanker for the New Zealand Secondary Schools team for a game against Samoa Schools in Wellington, and three matches in Australia. Other future All Blacks in the squad were Isaia Toeava (De La Salle College, Auckland), Hika Elliot (Hastings Boys' High School), captain Jamie Mackintosh (Southland Boys' High School), and Jeremy Thrush (Hutt Valley High School.)

The 'test' of the tour was the final match against Australia Schools in Brisbane. Read appeared as a substitute in the 18–16 win.

In 2004, having finished secondary school, Read chose to travel the relatively short distance down State Highway 1 to study at Waikato University in Hamilton. The time had also come when he had to choose between the summer and winter sports he excelled at. Trials for both the Under 19 cricket side and Under 19 rugby team were looming.

Given that the days of professional sport mean the possibility of a person representing their country in summer and winter codes now seems a thing of the past, Read passed up what dreams he may once have had to play for the Black Caps, and committed himself to rugby. He was chosen for the New Zealand Under 19s to play at the World Championship, which was held in South Africa that year. A large number of the squad had, like Read, progressed from the Secondary Schools side of the previous year.

Read's father, Terry, told Richard Knowler:

'We thought he would be a cricketer, but it didn't turn out that way. Northern Districts looked after him all the way through, but he just wanted to play rugby. He was determined, even back then, and gave as good as he got on the field. He wasn't the type to back down.'

The New Zealand team began with unbeaten matches against Ireland, Georgia and then

Australia. In the semifinal they faced determined hosts South Africa in Durban, and in a tight encounter eventually triumphed 30–23. The final against France saw the New Zealanders playing a much more dominant game. Read scored a try as they ran out winners by 34–11. He savoured winning his first international rugby trophy in a black jersey and being part of a side that was crowned World Champions. (Jeremy Thrush was named IRB U19 Player of the Year.)

The following year, Read was selected for the New Zealand Under 21 side to contest that age-group's annual World Championship, which was being held in Mendoza, Argentina. His former Secondary Schools teammates Thrush and Mackintosh were in the side, with the latter again captain. They were joined by the likes of Andy Ellis, Ben Franks, Hosea Gear, Richard Kahui and Liam Messam.

Just as for the All Blacks, New Zealand age-group rugby sides invariably enter competitions as the favourites, and the Under 21 team was expected to add another title to those won in 2000, 2001, 2003 and 2004. Things didn't go to plan when the team lost 43–46 to Australia in pool play, and 12–16 to South Africa in their semifinal. (The South Africans went on to beat Australia in the final.) Read played in all five matches, including the play-off for third against France, which was won 47–21, but he only started in one match — against Canada — at number eight.

The coach of the Under 19 side was BJ 'Aussie' McLean, who although born in Australia — hence his nickname — had grown up in Wellington, and settled in Christchurch to pursue a career as a rugby coach. Suitably impressed with the Read he coached and toured with, and convinced of his potential as a first-rate loose forward, he spoke to Canterbury coach, Rob Penney, who had himself been an uncompromising loose forward during

'You can play some pretty rough teams at times around here … but he was more the type to tell the hot-headed guys to pull their heads in.'

BJ 'Aussie' McLean

Canterbury's Ranfurly Shield heyday of 1982–85. (The Shield, known colloquially as the 'log o' wood', has been the most-prized provincial trophy in New Zealand rugby since it was gifted to the New Zealand Rugby Football Union by Governor General Earl Ranfurly in 1902.)

Read was offered a place in the Canterbury academy. A first-class rugby future lay ahead for him, although not wearing the red, black and white of Counties-Manukau, nor the blue-and-white hoops of Auckland, but rather the red and black of Canterbury.

'When a side like Canterbury is keen to have you down there,' said Read to Richard Knowler, 'you're not going to pass up an opportunity like that. They were really interested in me and showed a lot of intent in seeing me come down, whereas a few different teams up north didn't show the same amount of enthusiasm when looking at me.'

As he later told TV One, when he was growing up:

> *'Red and black would have been Papakura Rugby Club; [that's] probably the only team I would ever have imagined [playing for].'*

Read and girlfriend Bridget Funnell, who he had met at Rosehill College, packed up Read's little red car — how appropriate — and drove down to Christchurch. A career as a professional rugby player lay ahead.

Becoming a 'Cantab'

Once in Christchurch, Read began studying for a Bachelor of Sport Coaching at the University of Canterbury, turning out for the Canterbury University rugby club and acclimatising to the Christchurch weather. Read told the University of Canterbury student blog:

> 'The Canterbury Rugby Union put me up in this flat when I came down — a very cold old villa … It wasn't the best. So by the time it got into winter we had to move out. It was too cold!'

In April of 2006, two trials for the New Zealand Under 21 side were held in Porirua, just north of Wellington, in the form of games against the visiting Canada A team. Read played in the match that was won 36–0 by the 'Second Selection', scoring a try. To nobody's surprise, he was included in the Under 21 squad for the world championships for the second year in a row. Jamie Mackintosh again captained the team.

The tournament was held in France in June and it mirrored Read's and the team's experiences of the tournament the previous year in Argentina. They began by easily beating Italy (75–16), unconvincingly subduing England (29–14) and, as they had the year before, narrowly losing to Australia (17–21). This saw the side (again) line up against South Africa in the semifinals, which the South Africans won in good fashion (40–23). In the play-off for third, some revenge was exacted over Australia with a 39–36 victory. Read had played in all five games, but there was much disappointment that the team hadn't been able to improve on the previous year's third-place finish.

Looking back at Read's appearances in New Zealand age-group sides — Secondary Schools in 2003, Under 19s in 2004, and Under 21s in 2005 and 2006 — much could be said about his mental attitude, physical fitness and his playing ability in that he appeared in all 19 games, collectively, that those sides played.

Back in Christchurch, Read was selected in the 2006 Canterbury provincial squad, one of 44 players to appear in the 12 matches the province would play that year. Captained by Corey Flynn, the team began its season with two Ranfurly Shield defences. The first was an away game in Timaru against South Canterbury.

The second was at Jade Stadium in Christchurch against Wairarapa Bush. It was in that game that Read ran on for his first taste of New Zealand provincial rugby. The team from 'the Bush' was not expected to pose any real challenge to the holders, as they played in the lower Heartland competition. They began their challenge stoutly but Canterbury was quickly into try-scoring stride and the scoreboard ticked over with great rapidity. The final score was 96–10.

Kieran Read's First Provincial Game

Canterbury (Ranfurly Shield defence) versus Wairarapa Bush
Jade Stadium, Christchurch
12 July 2006

Canterbury won 96–10

Canterbury
Steven Yates, Nick Thomson, Tim Bateman, Mike Davis, Ben Nowell, Stephen Brett, Matt France, Peter Nixon, Hayden Hopgood (captain), Kevin O'Neill, Isaac Ross, Kieran Read, Campbell Johnstone, Tone Kopelani, Wyatt Crockett.
Reserves: Corey Flynn, Ben Franks, Craig Clarke, Mikaele Tuu'u, Kevin Senio, Hamish Gard, Casey Laulala.

Wairarapa Bush
Peato Lafaele, Lawrence Matthews, Tommy Harmon, Nathan Couch, Junior Tongia, Patrick Rimene, Hamish McKenzie, Sylvanus Iro, Mike Spence, Tomas Kedarabuka, Mike Robinson, Sam Henderson, Dylan Higginson, Joe Harwood (captain), Brett Rudman.

Read made seven more appearances for Canterbury (missing the match in which North Harbour won the Ranfurly Shield for the first time) before their season was ended in the quarterfinals of the Air New Zealand Cup with a loss to Wellington. Read's first try came against Counties-Manukau, his old province.

During this season, he met Canterbury Crusaders coach Robbie Deans for the first time, and was somewhat surprised when Deans told him he would be in his Super Rugby squad come the end of the year.

Deans, a former fullback, was something of a local legend, having played 146 times for Canterbury between 1979 and 1990, scoring 1641 points. He represented the All Blacks in five tests and 10 tour games from 1983 to '85. He had begun coaching the Canterbury provincial team in 1997 (with Steve Hansen, who had also played for Canterbury as a midfield back, as assistant). In 1998, Deans became manager of the Crusaders, who were coached by another former teammate, Wayne Smith. He stepped into the role of coach in 2000 when Smith was appointed coach of the All Blacks.

As the 2006 Air New Zealand Cup headed towards a conclusion, *New Zealand Herald* writer David Leggat cast his eye over young players who had opportunities in the spotlight due to the absence of All Blacks who were committed to the Tri-Nations campaign. Leggat looked well into the future to highlight players he considered would be part of the World Cup campaign in 2011. He profiled four individuals. One was Read, who Leggat described as a 'strong, rangy Papakura-born loose forward who has all the hallmarks of being an All Black-in-waiting'. The others profiled were all backs: wing David Smith (Auckland), speedster Lelia Masaga (Counties-Manukau), and centre Richard Kahui (Waikato).

Leggat was not the only rugby scribe

Jamie Mackintosh

Robbie Deans

impressed with the play of Read. The editors of *The SKY Sport Rugby Almanack of New Zealand* named him as one of their five Promising Players of the Year, alongside Nick Crosswell (Manawatu), Israel Dagg (Hawke's Bay), David Smith (Auckland), and age-group teammate Jeremy Thrush (Wellington). Of Read they wrote:

> ' ... he has a physical presence on the field that, allied to speed, anticipation, correct decision making, good defence, good hands, says he has a lot going for him. It is over to [him] to capitalise on a good start.'

That 'good start' was built upon the following year with Read indeed being named by coach Robbie Deans in his 35-man Crusaders squad for the 2007 Rebel Sport Super 14 Championship. It was Deans' eighth year at the helm of the franchise, during which time they had won the title three times (2002, 2005 and 2006), lost the final three times (2000, 2003 and 2004), and made the semifinals once (2007). Such an enviable record meant the team was seen as setting the benchmark in Super Rugby. Richie McCaw was to captain the team, as he had done since 2005.

But controversially missing from the line-up at the beginning of the season were All Blacks from both squads. At the instruction of All Blacks coach Graham Henry, and in agreement with the New Zealand Rugby Union, the players were being rested as part of a 'conditioning window' in preparation for the World Cup later in the year. The absences contributed to the Crusaders having 13 new players in their squad, many of whom had no experience of the next level of professional rugby. This was a matter of some concern to Deans, who commented in his biography *Robbie Deans: Red, Black and Gold* by Matt McIlwraith that:

> '… it meant taking a few gambles on players. Not so much on their ability, but on their temperament, and their ability to step up. The situation also meant that some players were going to have to be promoted a little bit earlier than we had originally planned.'

So much so that, in Read's case, he not only played in pre-season games, he even captained one of the sides. It was an immediate signal from Deans that he had confidence in Read to not only be part of his team, but also to be one of the leaders.

The trust placed in Read by Deans came as a surprise to some of his teammates, including McCaw. But he, like so many others, quickly saw why Deans had faith in the dedicated young loose forward, as he later told reporter Toby Robson:

> 'He [Read] picked things up pretty quick, which is always a good sign. He was always on the ball and, because of that, he earned the trust and respect of the guys who had been around very quickly … he also had a very good rugby brain on him and knew the right time to do things.'

Read's maturity was such that he was also included in the Crusaders' strategy group. Now he could view the game not only from the position of an individual with a core role and function, but also from a wider team

---

Kieran Read's First Super Rugby Game

Crusaders versus Blues
Eden Park, Auckland
2 February 2007

Crusaders lost 25–34

Crusaders
Brent Ward, Rico Gear, Caleb Ralph, Casey Laulala, Scott Hamilton, Stephen Brett, Andrew Ellis, Mose Tuiali'i, Johnny Leo'o, Kieran Read, Kevin O'Neill, Ross Filipo, Campbell Johnstone, Corey Flynn (captain), Ben Franks.
Reserves: Ti'i Paulo, Wyatt Crockett, Jake Paringatai, Peter Nixon, Kevin Senio, Tusi Pisi, Rua Tipoki.

Blues
George Pisi, Doug Howlett, Isaia Toeava, Sam Tuitupou, Anthony Tuitavake, Isa Nacewa, David Gibson, Jerome Kaino, Daniel Braid, Angus Macdonald, Troy Flavell (captain), Greg Rawlinson, John Afoa, Derren Witcombe, Saimone Taumoepeau.
Reserves: Rudi Wulf, Luke McAlister, Steve Devine, Justin Collins, Anthony Boric, Nick White, Chris Heard.

The Crusaders' horsemen, a long-standing pre-match feature of the franchise's home games.

perspective. What had been largely instinctual in his rugby game up until then became a little more studied and refined.

His Crusaders debut proper came against the Blues at Eden Park on 2 February 2007 as Crusader number 110, in front of a crowd of over 26,000 people. The game, played at a great pace on a warm, still Auckland evening, was won by the Blues, 35–24. The Crusaders, lacking seven of their All Blacks (which meant Corey Flynn took over as captain in place of McCaw), were left rueing their poor defensive lines and missed tackles, which allowed the Blues backs to frequently make quick territorial advances and score tries.

By Round 7, Richie McCaw and fellow loose forward Reuben Thorne (a former All Black captain) were allowed to play again and Read found himself taking the field from the bench, from where he had a noticeable impact. The Crusaders had a mixed season, winning just eight of their 14 games. They did, however, make the semifinals, but lost to the Bulls 12–27 in Pretoria. No tries were scored by either side, with the Bulls' Derick Hougaard dominating from the kicking tee with eight penalty goals (and a dropped goal). A week later, the Bulls beat the Sharks 20–17 to win the final, the first time in six years that no New Zealand team had contested the final.

Looking back on Read's first campaign for the Crusaders, Deans said:

'We always knew he was going to be a gem, but the circumstances meant he ended up carrying a bigger load starting off than he might have done otherwise. But he handled it so well, he wound up playing every game that year and hasn't looked back.'

Two weeks after the match in South Africa, Read was again globetrotting, slotting onto the side of the Junior All Blacks scrum for their first match against Samoa in the 2007 IRB Pacific Nations Cup in Apia. The shortlived tournament also featured Fiji, Japan, Tonga and, for the first time, Australia A, and matches were played at a multitude of venues around the Pacific with the Junior All Blacks travelling from Apia to Suva, then Nuku'alofa, Dunedin and, finally, Tokyo.

Competition for starting places was strong, particularly in the loose forwards, which, as well as Read, featured team co-captains Daniel Braid and Marty Holah, as well as Jerome Kaino and Canterbury teammate Mose Tuiali'i. (All would play for the All Blacks at some stage in their rugby careers.)

Read was in the starting line-up for the games against Samoa and Tonga and came on as a substitution against Japan. The Junior All Blacks team won the tournament and was unbeaten in the five games. The highlight of the series for them was undoubtedly the 50–0 thrashing of Australia A in Dunedin. Of the 30 players in that Juniors All Blacks squad, only five did not go up to the next level — to play for the All Blacks.

A month after that island-hopping event, Read was back in red and black, turning out for Canterbury as a blindside flanker in the Air New Zealand Cup.

Since being won by North Harbour the previous season, the 'log' had moved on from Harbour (who repelled three challengers) to Waikato. Cantabrians were delighted when the national championship game in Hamilton for their table-topping side became a Shield challenge.

In the clash, Canterbury ran in five tries — four in the first 20 minutes — which completely knocked the stuffing out of the Waikato side. First five-eighth Stephen Brett was lauded for his running play in the 33–20 victory, which gave Waikato the dubious honour of having equalled the then shortest reign as Shield holders at just seven days.

Hopes were high in Canterbury that it would be the dawn of another new and glorious Shield era for the province. It was not to be. After easily repelling the first challenge from Hawke's Bay 44–6, Canterbury lost their second defence three weeks later by 15–26 to an Auckland team coached by Pat Lam. In doing so, they also relinquished their spot at the top of the championship.

The team rebounded for its next match, which was the championship quarterfinal against Otago at Jade Stadium. The traditional southern rivals were sent back to Dunedin pondering just how they had been thrashed 44–6. Canterbury looked to have quickly regained form.

Their semifinal was against Wellington who they had beaten by 41–23 earlier in the competition. There's an old saying that form counts for nothing in play-off games, and Wellington proved this, winning in Christchurch 26–21. The team from the capital would go on to lose the final to Auckland at Eden Park.

On 12 October 2007, Read's first 10-month 'season' as a professional rugby player was over. He had scored six tries, appeared in all 14 Crusaders games, three of the five Junior All Blacks matches and all 13 Canterbury games. Across the board, rugby pundits were pointing to him as a sure-fire bet to make the All Blacks. It was just a question of when. Events taking place on the other side of the world during the latter stages of the Air New Zealand Cup appeared to make his selection seem likely sooner rather than later.

Graham Henry knew Read could be an All Black, but also that he had the potential to be a great All Black.

A World Cup Disaster

Graham Henry now admits that the 'conditioning window' that saw some All Blacks missing from the initial rounds of the 2007 rugby competition, in order to keep them fresh for the Rugby World Cup, was a mistake. For the first time since 2001, no New Zealand franchise made the Super Rugby final and there was some disgruntlement from players, who wanted to be playing the game they loved and were paid to play, and from coaches, who were not able to select their leading players.

Certainly, the All Blacks looked sharp and in great physical condition when they began their 2007 World Cup campaign with a win against Italy 76–14 in the French city of Marseille. There were further romps against Portugal (108–13), Scotland (40–0), and Romania (85–8). Their style of play was entertaining, accurate and fast-paced, but there were concerns that the perennial cup favourites were not being tested enough before the play-off rounds.

The match against Scotland had a farcical element to it in that both sides wore jerseys that, in the gloom of Edinburgh's Murrayfield Stadium, were almost indistinguishable in colour, with the All Blacks wearing an alternate silver-grey strip and Scotland a blue-grey jersey. At times, the confusion between who was on which side drew out hapless frustration in the reactions of All Blacks playmakers. Permission was granted for the All Blacks to change back to a different-coloured jersey at half-time. The only problem was that, understandably, they hadn't brought any with them to the match.

The cup competition itself took an unexpected turn when Argentina beat hosts France 17–12 in pool play. This meant that the All Blacks' quarterfinal opponents at the Millennium Stadium in Cardiff would not be the expected South Americans, but their unpredictable World Cup nemesis, France, who had — by fair means and foul — completely thrown the All Blacks off their game in the 1999 World Cup semifinal to win by 40–23 (after the All Blacks had earlier been leading 24–10).

As play unfolded in the quarterfinal, it turned out there was another unknown at Cardiff: young referee Wayne Barnes. The All Blacks, again playing in their alternate strip, were beginning to suppress the French challenge and, with 10 minutes to go in the first half, were leading 13–0. It was at around this time that the All Blacks

The 2007 Rugby World Cup campaign began under sunny skies, but gloom would soon descend.

saw the last of the penalties awarded to them, despite a litany of infringements that were all too easy for the broadcast audience to see. The tide turned.

A yellow card to Luke McAlister and the departure due to injury of first-fives Dan Carter and Nick Evans were unforeseen disruptions, but ones the All Blacks had to overcome. With the score at 13–13, the forwards were doing their best to engage the French forwards and create space for the backs. But, despite blatant hands in the ruck and offside play by the French, no recriminations came from Barnes, nor his side-line assistants.

The tireless Rodney So'oialo scored an unconverted try to make the score 18–13 in favour of the All Blacks. But with just over 10

minutes to play, disaster struck. Yannick Jauzion, whose Academy Award-quality theatrics had seen McAlister sin-binned for knocking him over as he chased a kick, scored a try. It looked like a piece of traditional French backline flair except for one thing. One of the passes had been so far forward that even some British rugby writers who delight in All Black misfortune struggled to call it marginal. With the try converted, the French were ahead by 20–18, much to the bewilderment of the All Blacks on the field, the coaches sitting in the open stand, and the fans in the stadium, listening to commentary on radio, or watching the match on televisions around the world.

Try as they might, the All Blacks were fighting the slipping tide of time left on the clock, and the

The late great Jerry Collins on the rampage against Portugal, Rugby World Cup, 2007.

inability of Barnes to raise his arm in their favour. A panicky, long-range attempted dropped goal by McAlister summed up the last few minutes of the match. Almost a minute after 80 minutes ticked over on the official clock, the All Blacks were still trying to create an opportunity to score but were barely making it beyond the halfway line. Andrew Hore made a charge, but had the ball stripped as he fell to ground, and the French halfback Elissalde ran from one side of the field towards the side-line of the other and kicked the ball so hard into the stands it is amazing it didn't blow a hole in the stadium wall! The final whistle sounded. The French had upset the All Blacks again.

The All Blacks and management … well, they were downcast and struggling to comprehend what had occurred in a match veteran rugby writer Bob Howitt described as 'a bizarre contest' in his biography, *Graham Henry: Final Word*.

The players' reactions were no better illustrated than when a TV camera focused on the injured Dan Carter and the subbed Byron Kelleher sitting in the stands. They looked absolutely stunned, struggling to reconcile their World Cup exit with just how it came to be.

Immediately, sections of the media and fans began their attacks on the character of Graham Henry (particularly) and his team, mirroring the abhorrent behaviour that had been seen in response to losses in the two previous cups.

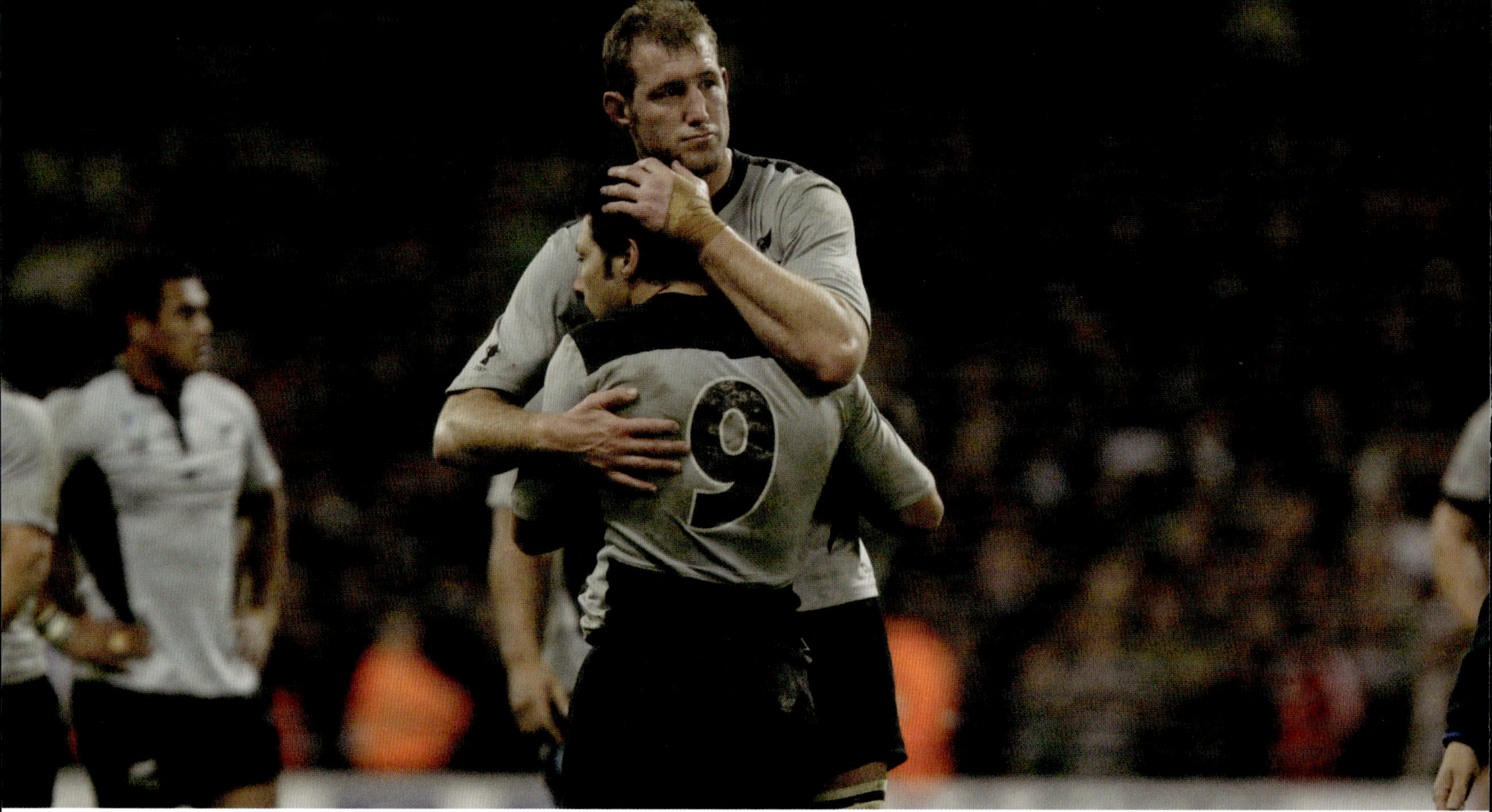
9

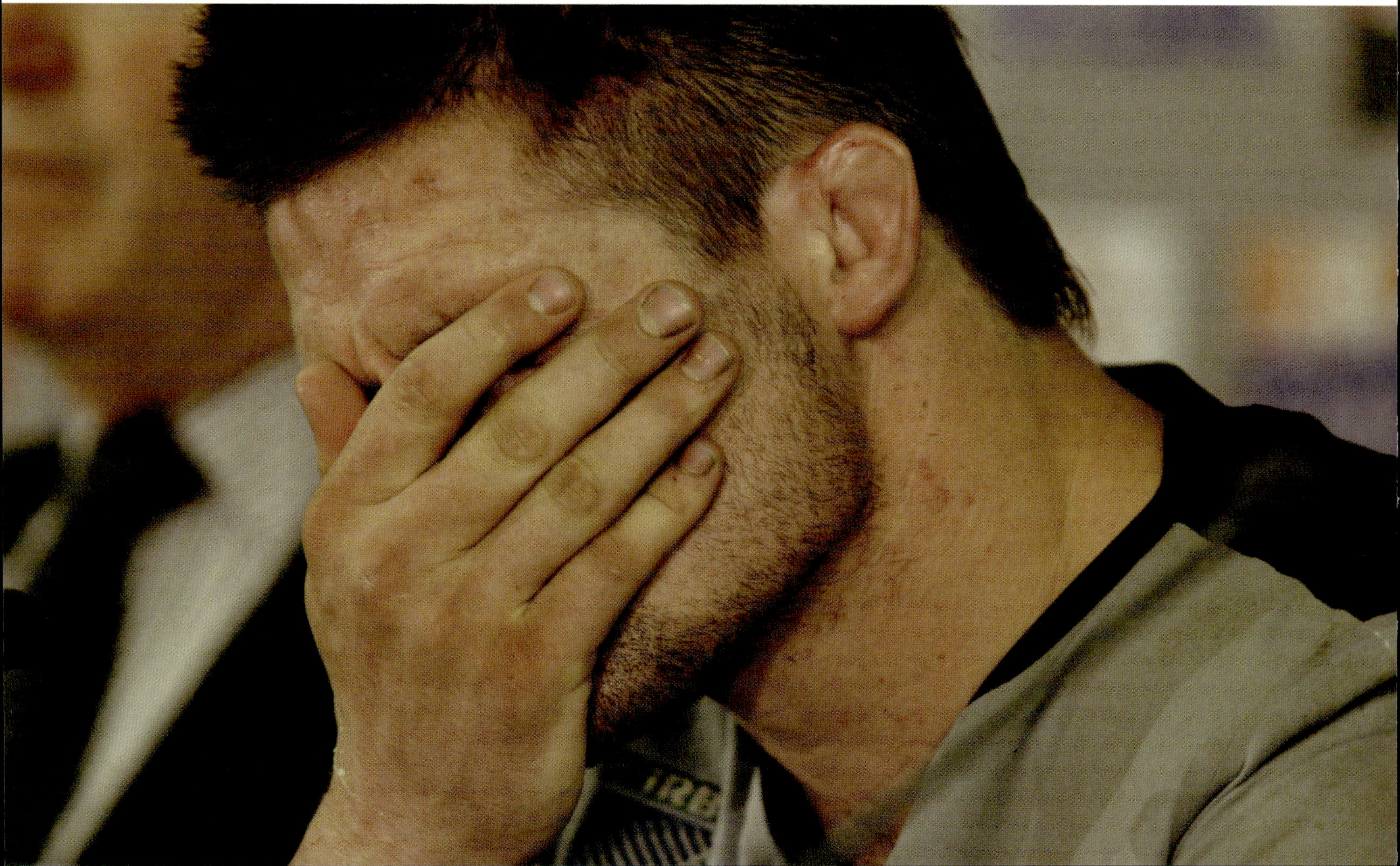
IRB

But those losses had been in the semifinals. This quarterfinal loss was the All Blacks' worst result at a Rugby World Cup. Talkback radio callers and hosts called for Henry to be sacked. Some of the players worried about how they would be received when they got back to New Zealand.

The Rugby World Cup cycle of four years invariably sees the retirement of senior players from all nations, planned and announced in advance of the tournament, and at its conclusion. Contracts for large salaries are signed with overseas clubs and preparations made to set up new homes overseas.

The 2007 cup was no different for New Zealand, with a host of senior players heading to new rugby pastures at the tournament's completion. Some rugby writers have suggested the individual plans of some players were a distraction during the campaign. One who wasn't on the departure list was Rodney So'oialo, who had not received half the criticism for his play in the semifinal that some of his teammates endured. His time as the incumbent number eight, which began in 2004, two years after his All Black debut, looked set to continue.

But immediately after the cup shock, all the focus was on Henry and whether he should reapply, let alone be reappointed, to the position of head coach.

Henry, who had said previously that he should be judged on the World Cup, did reapply, basing his presentation to the New Zealand Rugby Union selection panel largely on the repetitious errors of Barnes and his officials during the Cardiff match. His main rival for the post was Crusaders coach Robbie Deans. He saw a tide of public and media support come in behind him in the months following the loss to France. Many saw him as a shoo-in, but there was a surprise in store.

Henry was reappointed.

Deans and his supporters were dismayed. But then he provided a shock of his own. He had been headhunted to become the new coach of arch-rivals, the Wallabies.

For the media, this was manna from heaven. Come the Tri-Nations, the controversially reappointed Henry would be up against the rejected Deans.

During Deans' last Super Rugby campaign with the Crusaders, Kieran Read was hugely impressive, playing mostly at blindside flanker as the Crusaders won their seventh Super Rugby title. They lost only two matches (to the Chiefs and Highlanders) and defeated the Waratahs in the final at Christchurch by 20–12, a fitting farewell to the departing Deans, who had been head coach of the Crusaders for 119 games. Read had played with what was becoming his trademark dynamism in all 15 games as part of a potent loose forward trio, alongside McCaw and Tuiali'i.

Surely Read would now be the logical loose forward back-up for the All Blacks? The Chiefs' Sione Lauaki, despite having great speed for a very big man, was proving erratic on and off the field. His teammate Liam Messam was another contender, while Tuiali'i hadn't played for the All Blacks since 2006 and was preparing for a move to the lucrative corporate club scene in Japan.

Many of the rugby public, and especially those in Canterbury, were gobsmacked when Henry didn't include Read in his All Blacks squad for the four Iveco home tests against Ireland, England (two) and Samoa, nor the following Tri-Nations series (which the All Blacks won despite two losses to South Africa). Naturally, Read himself was

Left: Despair in Cardiff. At the final whistle (top) and as Richie McCaw faces the media (bottom).

A familiar sight in the 2000s — the Crusaders as Super Rugby champions.

disappointed and among those who called him to commiserate was Deans, who was about to name his first Wallaby squad. The Crusaders mentor intimated that Read's time would come and that he just had to keep playing like an All Black.

Certainly, So'oialo continued to play well, and, in fact, seemed to be getting more astute on the field. This was acknowledged by the All Black selectors when he was appointed captain after McCaw injured his ankle in the first test against England and he led the side until McCaw's return late in the Tri-Nations campaign. However, his fearless physical commitment had some observers wondering how much longer his body could endure the demands of top-level rugby.

Henry told questioning media that Read was deserving of a rest, but the underlying reason appears to have been that the selectors had noticed a physical flaw in Read's play. While possessed of great stamina and upper body strength, the view was that he wasn't harnessing the potential power of his legs.

Read hit the gym and then exhibited his new explosive power in captaining Canterbury in the Air New Zealand Cup. Naturally, he played in all 14 games as his side made the final against

Robbie Deans left New Zealand on a high, having clinched his fifth Super Rugby title.

the in-form, table-topping Wellington side (also the Ranfurly Shield holders at the end of the round-robin matches). He appeared to relish his position as captain, leading from the front with his quality play and decision-making, talking to individuals or the team when necessary, and engaging with referees in quietly persuasive and diplomatic fashion.

Expectations were high that the final would be a classic and that one of the key match-ups would be between the up-and-coming Read and the stand-in All Black captain, So'oialo. The weather gods had other plans for the night and

by the time the game kicked off, heavy wind and rain were battering Wellington and swirling about inside Westpac Stadium.

Canterbury edged out the favourites 7–6. With a smile a mile wide, Read, as Canterbury captain, received the silver trophy at the presentation ceremony and held it aloft. His team was the national provincial champions.

There was more delight the following day when he was included in the All Blacks squad for the end-of-year tour to the northern hemisphere. His time had come.

Man in Black

A year after playing for the Junior All Blacks, Read had joined the ranks of the senior team. When the excitement and multitude of congratulations from family and friends had settled down somewhat, Read began to plan for the trip.

'Five weeks is a long time to be away so it's good to get into the swing of things fast,' he wrote for allblacks.com. 'When I got the call-up to tour I wasn't too sure of what to bring on tour so I gave Richie [McCaw] a call and he filled me in.'

Two suitcases were packed: one for training, and the other for everything else.

The team was setting off with hopes of achieving another Grand Slam, which means tour wins against England, Ireland, Scotland and Wales. Henry's 2005 side had achieved the 'Slam', and the only other All Black side to do so was the 1978 team, led by captain Graham Mourie. That side had played 18 games, including the four test matches, on an eight-week tour.

By comparison, the 2008 itinerary saw the All Blacks lined up to play four tests and one rare non-international game against Irish provincial side, Munster.

The tour actually began in Hong Kong with a fourth Bledisloe Cup game of the year against Australia, and Read contributed a diary entry to allblacks.com, which included his observations of the city and how good it was to have his own room 'because there's no arguing over the remote, or snoring issues'! He also gave a brief rundown of the afternoon's training session:

> 'We had training at So Kon Po Ground which is across the road from Hong Kong Stadium and that went pretty well. The heat hits you and you lose a few kilos of sweat so we need to drink plenty of water. I was wearing a monitor that measures the effort I put in so I think I went a little harder than normal. After training we were driven to a club with a pool on the roof. I'm not a swimmer so I just relaxed and threw a ball around — that was until the lifeguards told us off and that put an end to the throwing.'

Read watched from the stands as his teammates won a tight encounter 19–14, in front of nearly 40,000 spectators. They then left the humidity of South Asia for the cold of a deepening northern hemisphere winter.

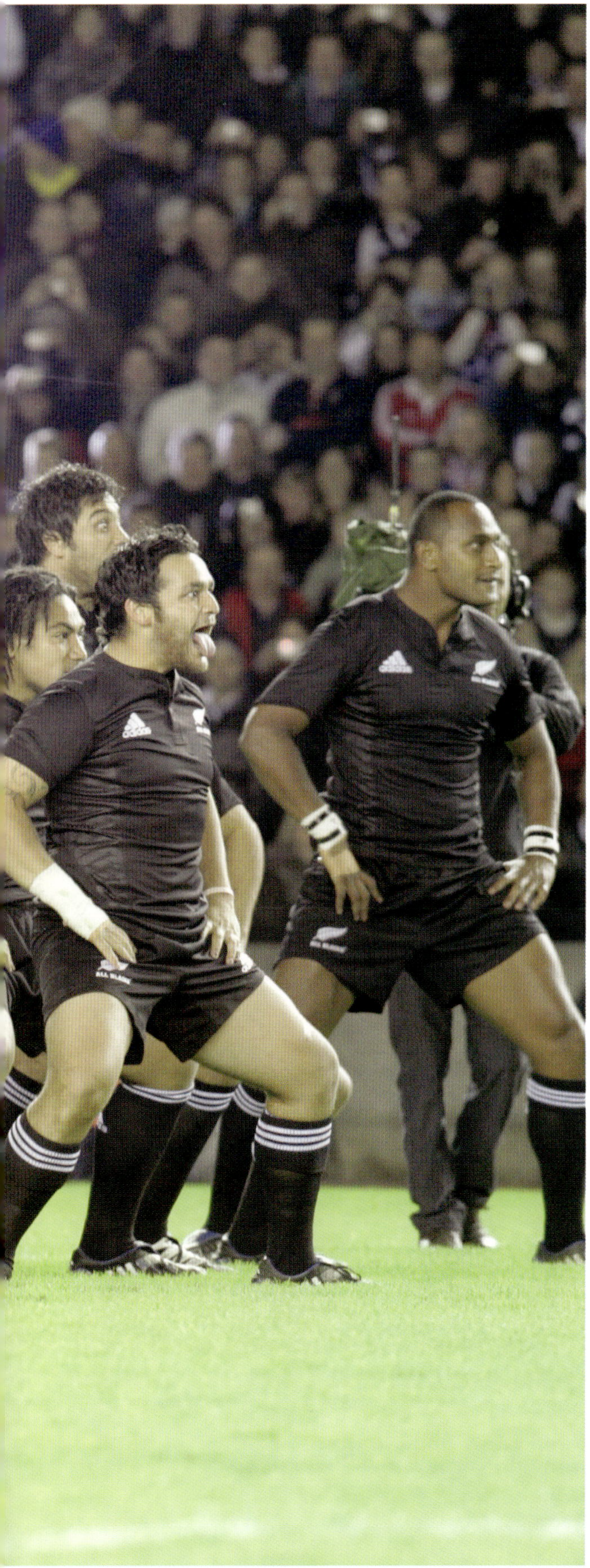
adidas

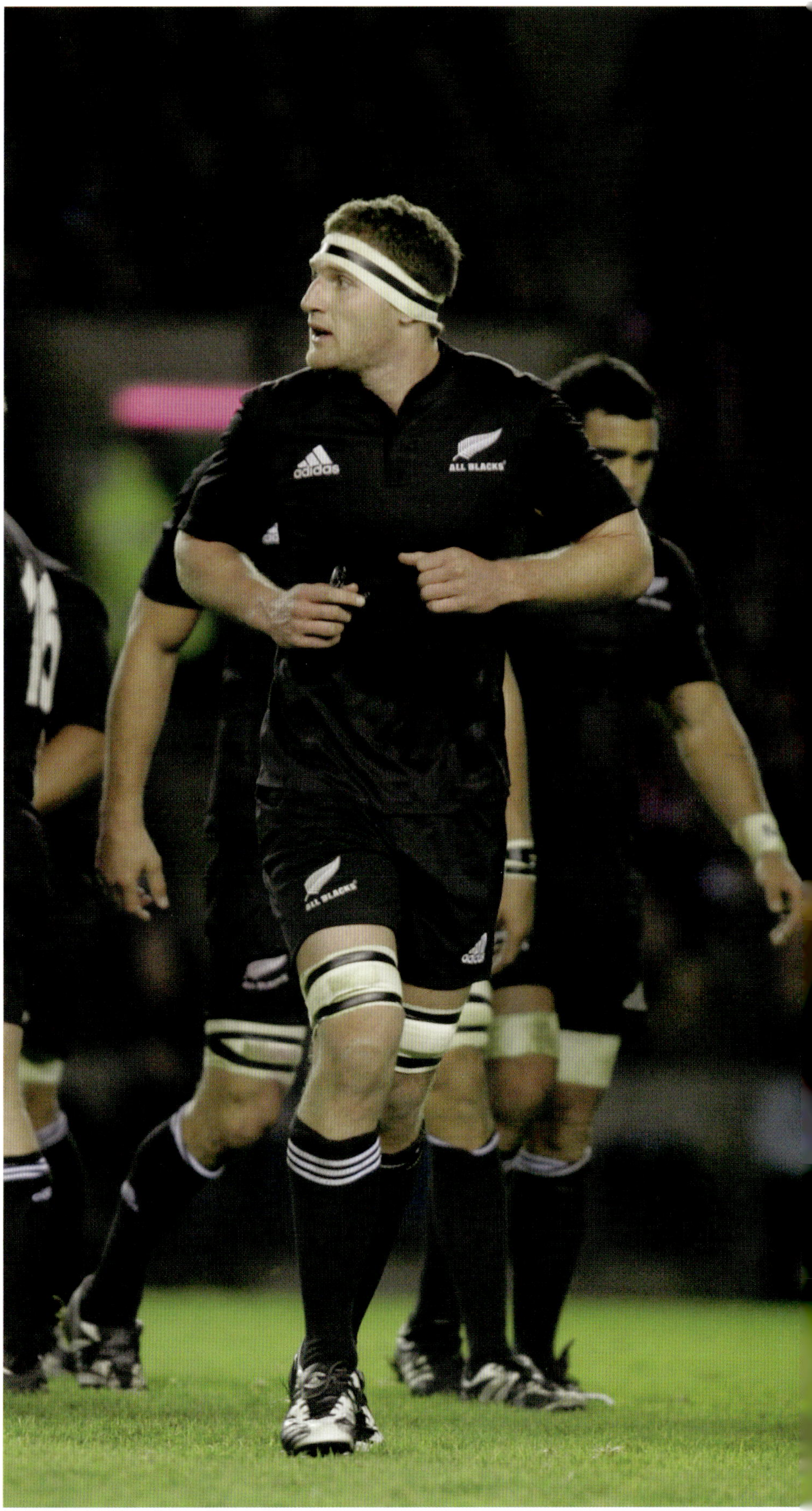
adidas
ALL BLACKS

Read's All Black debut came wearing the number six jersey in the first game up north, against Scotland in Edinburgh on 8 November 2008. Walking onto the Murrayfield pitch in front of nearly 52,000 spectators on a cold, clear night, he became All Black number 1083. None who had preceded him in the black jersey had ever experienced a loss to Scotland since the two teams first met in 1905 (though there had been two draws, in 1964 and 1983). Thus the selectors fielded what was considered by many commentators to be a second-string team for the All Blacks' 441st test. Also making their All Black debuts that night, under the captaincy of Keven Mealamu, were Liam Messam and Read's age-group teammate from as far back as the New Zealand Secondary Schools 2003 side, Southland's Jamie Mackintosh.

The Scots played with traditional early vigour and determination, but by half-time the All Blacks had scored two tries to lead by 18–6. The second of those tries, scored by Piri Weepu, was the 1500th scored by the All Blacks in tests, the first having been way back in 1903 against Australia.

The second half remained a contest but the All Blacks made more of their opportunities, scoring two more tries, and the match was whistled to a close by referee Wayne Barnes with the score at 32–6.

Read had at last experienced rugby at the highest level and joined that very select and exalted group of men known as All Blacks.

The following week, Read was a late substitution in the 22–3 win against Ireland at Croke Park in Dublin. The match was played at the home of traditional Gaelic games (hurling and Gaelic football) while the traditional home of Irish rugby, Lansdowne Road, underwent a major reconstruction, becoming Aviva Stadium. Notably, the capacity at Croke Park was considerably greater than at the rugby venue.

Kieran Read's Debut All Blacks Game

New Zealand versus Scotland
Murrayfield, Edinburgh
8 November 2008

New Zealand won 32–6

All Blacks
Jamie Mackintosh, Keven Mealamu (captain), John Afoa, Anthony Boric, Ali Williams, Kieran Read, Adam Thomson, Liam Messam, Piri Weepu, Stephen Donald, Joe Rokocoko, Ma'a Nonu, Richard Kahui, Anthony Tuitavake, Isaia Toeava.
Reserves: Corey Flynn, Neemia Tialata, Ross Filipo, Richie McCaw, Andy Ellis, Dan Carter, Cory Jane.

While the general spectator seating was of a poorer quality than that at many major modern rugby stadia, one of the talking points for the players was the enormous chandelier made of Waterford crystal that hung in the players' bar.

Three days later, Read played his only non-international game for the All Blacks on a night that was a very special occasion for the province of Munster in the south of Ireland.

On 31 October 1978, the red jerseys of Munster became the first (and only) Irish team to beat the All Blacks. They triumphed 12–0, thanks in part to their relentless tackling, at Thomond Park in Limerick. A number of All Blacks involved in the loss later said, in very deadpan fashion, that they were so outdone by the home side that they were lucky to get zero!

Thirty years later — to commemorate that famous game — and on an icy, clear night, the All Blacks experienced the almost ferocious

The 2008 midweek All Blacks prepare to face Munster.

passion of Munster again. Piri Weepu captained the team, which gave the haka some added mana, but then came the real surprise of the night: Munster responded with a haka of its own! Why was an Irish team responding to the All Blacks challenge with its own haka? Because the team included four Kiwis, notably former flying All Black winger and record try-scorer Doug Howlett, and centre Rua Tipoki.

For the next 80 minutes of play the crowd roared themselves hoarse as the Munstermen took the game to the All Blacks. At half-time, the home team led the visitors by 16–10. Was history going to repeat itself?

Ten minutes after half-time, Read came on as a substitute and found himself in the midst of rugby's version of an arm wrestle. Each time the All Blacks looked as though they might be gaining some ascendancy, the men of Munster regrouped and took the game to the All Blacks

Ex-pats Jeremy Manning and Rua Tipoki lead the 'Munster haka'.

again. Several penalty chances, which would have given the All Blacks the lead, were missed by Stephen Donald. All the while the clock ticked down, watched and willed on by 27,000 fans who grew ever more expectant of a great upset.

That was until, with three minutes to go, Joe Rokocoko scored the try that sealed the game for the All Blacks. They had won 18–16, but were full of praise for their opponents who gave the 23 All Blacks who took the field that night a taste

of days gone by. That is, when All Blacks went on long tours, and when midweek, non-test match encounters could be every bit as challenging as Saturday test matches.

The following week, the All Blacks beat Wales 29–9 in Cardiff. Ahead lay the final match of the tour against England at Twickenham on 29 November. The All Blacks were playing to secure their Grand Slam and to retain the Hillary Shield, named in honour of Sir Edmund Hillary and

Hosea Gear (above) and Joe Rokocoko found the spirited Munster defence hard to break at Thomond Park, until the 75th minute.

played for between New Zealand and England.

Read replaced Kaino on the side of the scrum early in the second half. On a drizzly afternoon the All Blacks scored three tries and Carter kicked five penalties as the All Blacks comfortably won the match 32–6. The English seemed determined to play negatively and this led to referee Alain Rolland of Ireland sending four of the men in white to the sin bin during the match. For almost half of the game, England was only playing with 14 men. The win meant that the 2008 All Blacks became known as the Third Grand Slam team.

On a personal note, it had been an amazing year of rugby for Read. He had played in a Crusaders side that took out the Super 14 championship, and had captained Canterbury to win the national championship. To top it all off, he now had four All Black games to his name and was part of a Grand Slam-winning squad. His year was recognised by the editors of the *Rugby Almanack of New Zealand*, who included him in their Almanack New Zealand XV of the Year, albeit as back-up to So'oialo. But Read's star was on the ascendant.

Joe Rokocoko saved the day for the All Blacks and broke the hearts of Munster fans.

Being an All Black Isn't Easy

Less than three months after the 2008 All Black tour ended, the Super 14 resumed. But for players such as Read, there was little rest once the New Year began. The Crusaders squad worked on its fitness, with gut-busting runs up the Port Hills, and practice matches before the first round in the middle of February. Read took his place at blindside flanker, as Thomas Waldrom had moved down from Wellington to replace Tuiali'i at number eight. The team had a new coach, too, with former All Black and Crusaders captain Todd 'Toddy' Blackadder replacing the departed Robbie Deans.

With Carter absent due to his sabbatical in France at the Perpignan club, during which time he ruptured his Achilles tendon, and with injuries and concussion disrupting McCaw's appearances, the Crusaders lost three of their first four matches. Against the Highlanders in Dunedin they secured a bonus point without scoring any points! The 0–6 loss brought back memories for older rugby fans of days gone by when such scores were commonplace. However, the Crusaders recovered their form and made the play-offs, winning eight of their next nine games before falling 23–36 to the Bulls in their semifinal in Pretoria.

The 2009 international home series got off to a bad start for the All Blacks and for Read (who was in the starting line-up) when the visiting French team won the first test in Dunedin 27–22. While it had long been part of rugby folklore that the All Blacks tend to splutter their way to wins at the very start of home test series, few expected the tourists (captained by Thierry Dusautoir and coached by Marc Lièvremont) to begin their visit with a win. Since their first tour in 1961, they had only beaten the All Blacks in New Zealand three times — famously on Bastille Day 1978, and in the two 1994 tests. But the All Blacks line-up was missing a number of key players (McCaw, Ali Williams, Kaino, Carter, Sitiveni Sivivatu and Conrad Smith), and Luke McAlister was rushed back (albeit to the bench) after returning from playing club rugby in England. Mils Muliaina captained the side while Read, playing at blindside flanker, formed the loose forward trio with Adam Thomson (7) and Liam Messam (8).

In the wet at Carisbrook it was acknowledged

that the All Blacks pack lost the physical battle, and the French backs played with more cohesion than their All Blacks counterparts. A McAlister pass was latched onto by French fullback Maxime Médard, and he raced away for a try, which ultimately clinched the game for France.

In his appraisal of the match, *New Zealand Herald* rugby writer Wynne Gray wrote damningly that:

'The loose forwards struggled to make any impact but their ineffectiveness started with the lack of clout from the tight five. From there the inefficiency, ineptitude and inability to combat the Tricolores seeped through the side. The hosts failed to cope with the driving mauls of the French, they were buffeted in the collisions, bounced at the breakdowns, shunted off their ball at the scrums and snotted well behind the advantage line. It was a shabby start with little evidence they had a controlled plan to start the season.'

In other words, as captain Muliaina (who along with Joe Rokocoko and Tony Woodcock was a survivor from the 2007 World Cup quarterfinal) said, they were simply 'out-muscled'.

Coach Graham Henry gave all the credit to

Former All Blacks, Crusaders and Canterbury captain, Todd Blackadder took over as Crusaders coach following the departure of Robbie Deans.

Jubilation for France as they win the first test of the 2009 home series. The All Blacks were out-muscled, out-played.

France who had to make twice as many tackles, while the All Blacks were falling all too easily off theirs:

> 'We were second-best out there today and did not deserve to win. They were more physical than us.'

The All Black pack should not have been shown up as it was. It contained only one debutant — Isaac Ross at lock — but once the French sustained their impassioned start, it was hard for the All Blacks to get back into the game.

A week later in Wellington, they had their chance to prove that the still-stinging loss had been an aberration and retain the Dave Gallaher Trophy. (The silverware was named after the 1905 All Black captain, Gallaher, who had led the team on its first tour to England, Ireland, Scotland, Wales, France and North America. He captained the All Blacks in their first-ever test against France, in January 1906, which was also France's first international match. He went on to coach Auckland during the first great Ranfurly Shield tenure from 1908 to 1913, and was a selector for the All Blacks. In 1916, as World War One progressed, the Boer War veteran signed up, then tragically lost his life at Passchendaele in October 1917.)

Unsurprisingly, Henry made changes to the

George Whitelock succeeded Read as Canterbury provincial captain, and appeared in the Christchurch test against Italy in 2009.

side for the second test, including in the loose forwards. Tanerau Latimer came in for Thomson, Read moved to number eight in place of Messam, and was replaced by Kaino, who went into the blind-side flanker position.

As is so often the case in Wellington in June, the weather was atrocious and the ground particularly slippery. Strong winds swirled rain around the inside of the stadium, but both teams played as though conditions were much drier. The All Black forwards nullified much of the French muscle that had been their strength the week before and led 8–0 at half-time. Read came close to scoring and valiantly (but in vain) chased French wing Cédric Heymans, who scored a

dazzling try, skirting down the side-line past Cory Jane and Muliaina. The All Blacks won 14–10 but, to their disappointment, lost possession of the Dave Gallaher Trophy because of the points differential across the two matches: 36–37. They had missed out on holding on to the trophy by one point! But on the bright side, a win is a win, as they say.

The following week the team lined up against Italy (known as the 'Azzurri') in Christchurch. The All Blacks seemed to pick up where they had left off against the French. McAlister had a game that could politely be described as pretty awful. Credit must be given to the way the Italians played, led by inspirational captain and

number eight Sergio Parisse, but All Black errors meant the home side put a lot of pressure on themselves.

In one play, after a chip kick by Lelia Masaga (playing his only match for the All Blacks), Read dived on the loose ball in the Italian's in-goal area. He was confident of having scored a try but the video referee saw obstruction from Masaga and the try was disallowed.

With the All Blacks leading 13–3 at half-time, both teams essentially doubled their scores in the second half for the All Blacks to win by 27–6. It was another win for the All Blacks but, with the Investec Tri-Nations approaching, there was still much work to do.

The first match of that tournament was against Australia, at Eden Park, with Read dropping to the bench as McCaw and So'oialo returned to the side. For the Wallabies, their outstanding side-of-the-scrum forager George Smith was celebrating his 100th test appearance.

The match was a tense one and moments of individual brilliance by players on both sides were negated by a plethora of errors. At half-time an increasingly confident Australian side, hoping for its first win at the ground since 1986, was ahead by 13–10, having first scored a try after less than four minutes. But there were concerns about their scrum, which was being given a real going-over by the All Black pack. It was easy to quip that the Wallaby forwards could have been renamed 'backwards'! At the same time, the All Black lineout remained something of a mess, which was a worrying sight given they had three matches to play against the Springboks and their master lineout tactician Victor Matfield.

In the end, more accurate penalty kicking

George Smith, one of Australia's great open-side flankers.

Matt Giteau, Wallabies playmaker.

Victor Matfield wins yet another lineout.

by Stephen Donald than that of his opposite, Matt Giteau, proved the difference in the 'one try apiece' match. All Blacks 22, Australia 16.

Next stop South Africa. Read was on the bench (coming on after 53 minutes) as the All Blacks again started with Kaino, So'oialo and McCaw as their loose forwards. However, it was the South African number eight Pierre Spies who starred with his imposing play in the tight and speed in the loose, which saw rugby fans and writers in South Africa trumpeting their 'eightman' as the best in world rugby. The All Blacks, as they had in every international that season, struggled to play with any fluidity. The final score-line of 19–28 meant the South

Africans had their first-ever win over the All Blacks in Bloemfontein.

Things didn't get any easier the following week when the two teams met again, this time in Durban. The day belonged to Morne Steyn, who scored all of the Springboks' 31 points with eight (!) penalty goals, a try and a conversion. By half-time the score was 22–13 to South Africa. The All Blacks weren't playing accurately enough to pull off the counter-attacking plays they needed to in order to catch up on the board, and the match finished as another loss: 19–31.

The All Blacks had played six games in the 2009 international season and won only three. Though not an excuse for the hesitant, muddled

The Springboks celebrated three wins in a row against the All Blacks in 2009.

play of the All Blacks, one factor that may not be remembered by many is that the players were needing to get used to two sets of rules that year. That's right; in Super Rugby, what was known as the Experimental Law Variations (ELVs) were being trialled with a view to speeding up the game and rewarding teams that put their emphasis on attacking play to score tries, rather than defensive teams that constantly kicked high or downfield for position, hoping to draw penalties from the referee. Spectators had grown tired of games where what seemed like interminable periods were spent watching a game of 'force-back' with sides seemingly afraid to run the ball.

Come the international matches, the players had to revert to the regular laws, which still favoured unadventurous defensive sides. As skilled and adaptable as most All Blacks were, to play a dozen or more games under one set of rules for three months, and then have to revert back to older rules in crucial international fixtures, was a big ask.

What could not be excused were the lineouts, which had fans almost afraid to watch them as the horrors of that set piece from the early 2000s seemed to be rising up (pardon the pun) whenever it came time for the All Blacks to throw in the ball.

Read was back in the starting line-up for the

match against Australia at the ANZ Stadium in Sydney. In front of 80,000 people the All Blacks were down 3–12 at half-time but ground their way through to win the tight encounter 19–18, thanks to a Nonu try and four Carter penalties, the last just two minutes before fulltime. It broke their losing streak and put the Bledisloe Cup back in the cabinet for another year.

The next match a fortnight later was in Hamilton against the Springboks, who had the chance to become the top-ranked team in world rugby if they won, as well as be crowned Tri-Nations champions for the first time since 2004. Surprisingly, they had lost to Australia the week before, 21–6.

There was something of a media sideshow in the build-up to the Hamilton test with the Springboks choosing to stay and train in Auckland before undertaking the 90-minute drive to Hamilton on the day before the match. The reason? Coach Peter de Villiers told Australian reporters that 'There's nothing there.'

When asked for his views on Hamilton, Graham Henry looked mischievous as he smiled and said drolly, 'Best city in the world.'

Read again started at number eight, with So'oialo on the bench. But the All Blacks played as poorly as they had in the two earlier tests in South Africa and found themselves trailing at half-time by 12–22, an almost identical score to the Durban test. While the All Blacks' play was forgettable, the three booming, long-range penalty kicks from inside his own half by the Springbok Francois Steyn remain in many memories. Despite an exhilarating final few minutes during which McCaw scored a try from a deft Carter crosskick, the Boks were victorious, 32–29. For the first time since 1976, back in the days when the All Blacks undertook lengthy four-test tours of the Republic, they had beaten the men in black three tests in a row.

Graham Henry's after-match comments summed up not only the Hamilton game but the way the team had played all their games against the Springboks:

> 'They deserved to win. They played very structured rugby and played it very well. We didn't play well enough for the first sixty minutes. We needed to play for longer periods of time with a lot more consistency.'

In a *Herald* column, former All Black captain Sean Fitzpatrick didn't hold back on his thoughts about the set piece failures:

> 'In the first half it was just disgraceful. I don't know what they were doing. They [the All Blacks] trailed 12–1 in the lineouts at half-time. They had no idea where they were throwing it and the Springboks were totally dominating where New Zealand threw it.'

Assistant coach Steve Hansen had many fingers pointed at him for the lineout shambles. He believed the Springbok lineout dominance against all teams was due to the fact that:

> 'I don't think there's anyone under six foot two doing any lifting, particularly their back five; they're all very tall.

> Matfield's so good on his feet that he covers a lot of space. He puts himself in the game at lineout time by just getting up there. Half a lift from blokes that are as tall as they are, if you get it marginally wrong, then you're in trouble, whether it's your thrower, jumper or lifter.'

In the long-term, the observation would pay dividends for the All Blacks, but for now it just needed to be fixed.

Finally, on 19 September in Wellington, the All Blacks put together the performance they had been looking for all year. They crushed Australia 33–6 and Henry heaped post-match praise on the loose forward trio of McCaw, Read and Thomson:

> 'The work at the tackle area by the forwards in general, but particularly the loose forwards, was exceptional. We had a big game in the loose with Richie, Adam and Reado. They played well there, and were backed up by the tight five. We turned over a lot of ball and put the pressure on. We played well on attack and well on defence. It was a good all-round game.'

That last sentence is typical of Henry's understatement. It was a *great* all-round game, after weeks of lost opportunities due to poorly executed set piece plays and errors being made at crucial times.

Come the Air New Zealand Cup competition in August, George Whitelock was appointed Canterbury captain, as Read was on Tri-Nations duty with the All Blacks. He turned out only twice — against Waikato in Round 3, and Manawatu in Round 11. The invaluable Dan Carter was back in the Canterbury ranks for the first time since 2006, but it was a championship

The All Blacks had four Bledisloe Cup wins over Australia in 2009, the final encounter being played in Tokyo.

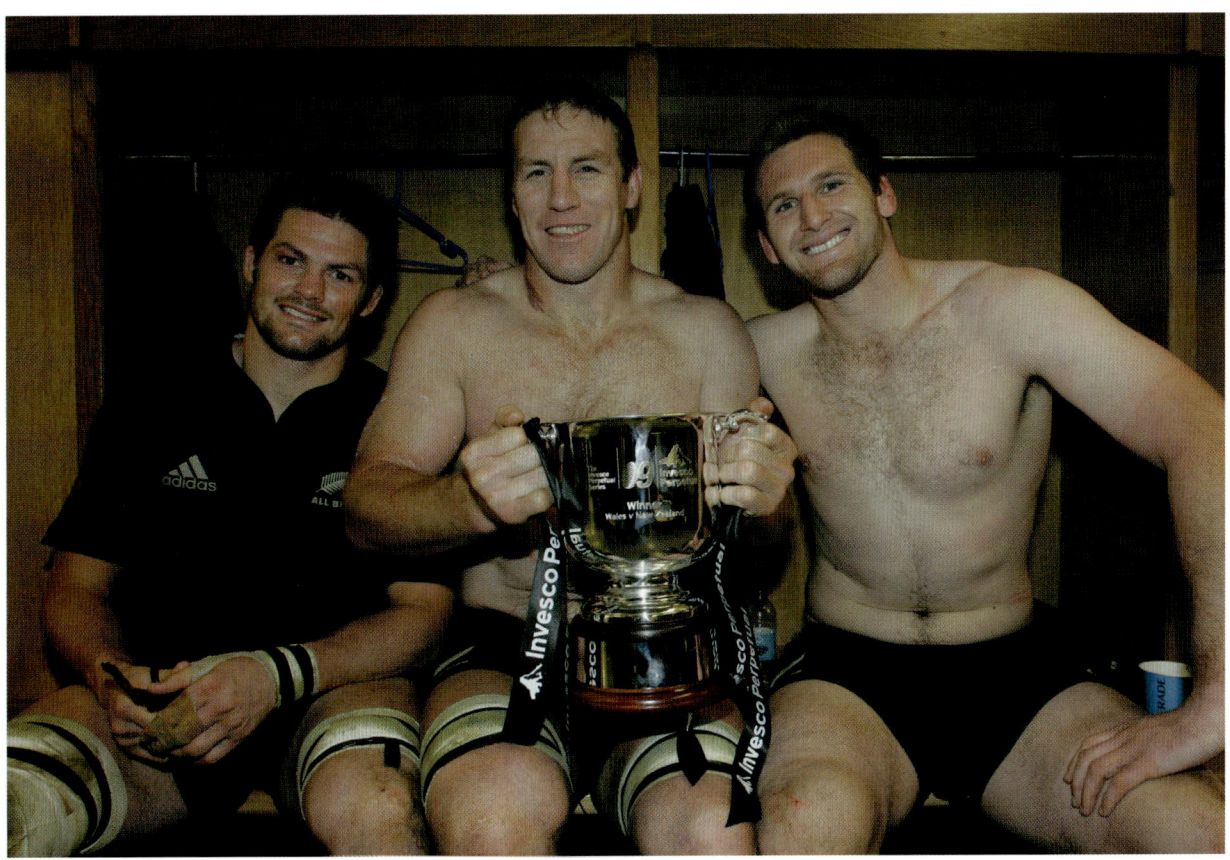

All smiles in the dressing rooom as Brad Thorn, flanked by McCaw and Read, holds the cup for winning The Invesco Perpetual Series against Wales.

of mixed fortunes for the team. They took the Ranfurly Shield off Wellington but then, after four defences, lost it to an in-form Southland who took it to Invercargill for the first time in 51 years. The national provincial final was again against Wellington but this time it was in Christchurch and Canterbury won 28–20.

Following the economic success of the previous year's match against Australia in Hong Kong, another Bledisloe Cup showcase was arranged for the All Blacks at the start of their northern hemisphere tour. At the end of October they played Australia in Tokyo, winning 32–19. So'oialo, following neck and shoulder injuries during the year, came back into the side in place of Read, with Henry pointing to Read's lack of

time on the field during the Air New Zealand Cup as a factor in his non-selection. The All Blacks won 32–19. It meant that Henry's All Blacks had swept Deans' Wallabies 4–0 that year.

The team then headed for Cardiff where they defeated Wales 19–12. The following week they were in Milan, beating Italy 20–6, the side being captained by Rodney So'oialo in what would be his final test for the All Blacks. England was overcome at Twickenham the following Saturday by 19–6. When journalists somewhat mischievously pointed out to assistant coach Steve Hansen that the All Blacks had only scored one try in each of the very stop-start matches, he replied, 'We haven't had the reward all tour, to be honest. That will come. If we keep

The 'captain's run' — final preparation before match-day.

knocking on the door, someone's eventually going to let us in.'

That someone was France, in arguably the best All Black performance of the year in Marseille on 28 November. With the Tricolores having beaten the Springboks two weeks earlier, the media was billing the match as the 'Battle of the Hemispheres'.

The All Blacks were looking to reclaim the Dave Gallaher Trophy and avoid losing to France for the third time in four outings. A quick glance at their rugby itineraries for the next two years would show their next clash would be at the Rugby World Cup in New Zealand in 2011, at which they would both be in Pool A.

In the days leading up to the match, the feeling in the All Black camp was one of confidence in their form and preparation. Read outlined his feelings on the captain's run at the Stade Vélodrome the day before the match for allblacks.com:

> 'The captain's run is a different training session to the rest of the week. It's more of a mental day really. We arrived at the stadium and Ricko [Richie McCaw] talked us through what plays we're going to run. DC [Dan Carter] had a big say in the session too because he'll be one of the main playmakers on the field for the match. It was all about staying fresh and sharp so we only ran

*about eighty per cent on the physical
side but a hundred per cent on the
mental side. We went through each of
our calls, just to make sure everyone's
got each move right in their head. I felt
happy calling, and making my calls in
the lineout too. I liked the feeling that
we just did the moves and did them
well. It was a good confidence run; it
went really smoothly. The Vélodrome is
a different kind of stadium compared to
the other ones we've played in on this
tour. It's an open air one. It's really going
to come to life tomorrow. I've heard that
there's usually a band playing and the
crowd chanting all the way through the
game when you play here. I've never
played in Marseille before, although I
have played age-grade rugby in France.'*
[Those games were for the New
Zealand Under 21s three years earlier.]

Conrad Smith scored one of the five tries in the great
All Black performance at Marseille in 2009.

After the initial quarter, which could be
characterised as a possession and territorial
dominance seesaw between the two teams,
the All Blacks stepped up the pace. The
forwards were running rampant and the backs
were finding gaps seemingly with ease. Five
unanswered tries were scored, to Jane, Kaino,
Muliaina, Sivivatu and Conrad Smith. It was an
exhilarating, resounding 39–12 victory. At the
final whistle the French crowd of over 60,000,
awed by the display the men in black had put on,
gave the All Blacks a standing ovation.

Henry told media:

*'This was a special day and a special
game. There has been a lot of boring
stuff played over the last couple of
years, but I think this was the best
attacking display by an international side
for some time. To play that well under
these rules is a difficult achievement.'*

With partner Bridget watching in the stands,
Read had arguably his best game in the All
Black jersey (on this occasion white jersey/the
alternate). His play was described by rugby writer
Marc Hinton as 'another eye-catching display'. He
was quick to the breakdown, won three lineouts
and carried the ball seven times.

After the match, McCaw was crowned IRB
World Rugby Player of the Year, and after another
of his extraordinary displays where he seemed
ever-present, no one could argue with that.

It was the end of the rugby season for Read
(who sat out the All Blacks' 18–25 loss to the
Barbarians at Twickenham). For the team, despite
winning 10 matches, it had been a frustrating

Read, Ellis and Kaino have the Dave Gallaher Trophy back in All Black possession.

few months when they knew they hadn't been playing to their potential and at times had struggled with the basics of the game. Criticism by the media and public had been quite harsh.

On an individual note, Read had supplanted So'oialo as the All Blacks' number one number eight. For the first time, he was named at that position in the New Zealand XV, chosen by the *SKY Sport Rugby Almanack*. His test cap tally now stood at 17, which included seven appearances from the bench. But he had played a part in all 13 All Black tests in 2009. In conjunction with Kaino and McCaw, and barring injuries and bad form, the next couple of years would give them the opportunity to establish themselves as the dominant loose forward trio in world rugby.

Player of the Year

The Crusaders kicked off their 2010 Rebel Sport Super 14 season with a 32–17 win against the Highlanders at AMI Stadium. Their run ended, once again, against the Bulls at the Orlando Stadium in Soweto, with a 24–39 loss. Just two weeks previously, the team had played the Bulls in Pretoria and controversially lost 35–40 after the final hooter had sounded, then flown back to Christchurch to play the Brumbies. They then had to fly back to South Africa again to play the Bulls for a place in the final.

Post-match, Bulls captain Victor Matfield, who was playing his 100th Super Rugby game, acknowledged the part such travel can play in finals matches:

'That's why you've got to have a home semifinal; it just improves your chances so much. Travelling like that can be very, very draining.'

McCaw, however, refused to blame their time spent in aeroplanes over the past fortnight:

'Today the guys were ready to play. We've got no excuses with the travel; we were ready to go and we came up short. I guess that's been the story of our season. We've had teams on the ropes and our mistakes let them off. In this competition you just can't afford to do that. The Bulls certainly made us pay for our mistakes tonight.'

The Bulls went on to beat the Stormers in the final, 25–17, giving them their third Super Rugby title in four years.

The Crusaders' team record was: played 14, won 8, lost 5, drawn 1 (26–26, against the Hurricanes in Wellington). Read played at both blindside and number eight in all but two of the matches.

His first international outing of 2010 was in the opening match of the Steinlager Series, in New Plymouth against Ireland, who were in the country for just one test before travelling across to Australia. While the All Blacks were in superb form, winning 66–28 with Read scoring one of the team's nine tries, the Irish cause was not helped when their number eight, Jamie Heaslip, was red-carded by referee Wayne Barnes. It happened after only 15 minutes of the game when Heaslip kneed McCaw — not once but twice — while McCaw was tangled up in a ruck.

Wales was the next opponent with tests in Dunedin (the last test to be played at Carisbrook) and Hamilton, the All Blacks winning both, 42–9 and 29–10.

Two home tests against South Africa commenced the Investec Tri-Nations competition. The South Africans were confident they could notch up a rare win at Eden Park after the trifecta of victories the previous year. On the contrary, the All Blacks were determined to put those results behind them. And that's just what they did, with one of those displays which seemed to typify their play at Eden Park in recent years. They matched the aggression of the Springbok forwards, with lock Brad Thorn having a particularly outstanding game, and the backs outplaying their opposites. South African number eight Pierre Spies was spoken of by his supporters and media as the Springboks'

most dangerous weapon, but he was largely anonymous compared with the energetic Read. Even the much-vaunted Springbok lineout was put under pressure by the All Blacks who were up by an incredible 20–3 at half-time, and ran out winners by 32–12.

Read, who seemed to never be out of shot in the television coverage, scored one of the four All Black tries, finishing a phase of play that typified the All Blacks' dominance up front and their willingness to pick and go. Inside the Springboks' 22-metre area, locks Tom Donnelly and Thorn both made ground towards the goal line. At a ruck beside the posts, Weepu stood up and sent a short pass to Read who had come

Israel Dagg tries to break the tackle of the Springboks' Schalk Burger, IRB Player of the Year in 2004.

charging in from five metres back. With perfect timing, he met the pass and dived across the line for a try.

The two sides then travelled to Wellington where the weather was dreadful. Despite the conditions, the final score was similar to that of the week before, 31–17, though things had been closer at half-time with the All Blacks taking a 13–7 lead.

Piri Weepu had one of his best games in the black jersey and a bearded Read seemed to be relishing the challenge of battling the large and much-hyped South African loose forward trio of Schalk Burger, Fritz Louw and Spies, taking the

attack to his opposites at every opportunity. Marc Hinton, writing for Stuff's *Rugby Heaven*, hailed Read, saying he:

> 'made a powerful start to this match, causing all sorts of problems with his mix of power and skilful offloads, and for the second straight week he played his highly rated opposite, Pierre Spies, off the park.'

Chris Matthews, reporting for TVNZ, gave his reaction to the game:

'If the Netherlands football team of the 'seventies gave the world "total football", then this All Blacks side is totally the rugby equivalent. The tempo Graham Henry's side plays with is a stunning advertisement for the game and another four-try bonus point, against a world class defence, is testament to that fact.'

The next match was against the Wallabies at Melbourne's Etihad Stadium, a free-flowing game that saw the All Blacks win comfortably. They had 32 points by half-time and won 49–28. In scoring one of their seven tries, McCaw set a new record for tries in test matches by an All Black forward — 16.

The return match was in Christchurch with the Wallabies looking to show they were a much better team than that humbled the week before. They attacked relentlessly but where the All Blacks' attacking mind-set had won the day the previous week, their defensive commitment this time shut out the Wallabies. New Zealand 20, Australia 10.

The All Blacks then headed for South Africa, teetering on the brink of securing another Tri-Nations title. They needed just one bonus point from their next two games. But, of course, they were playing for wins.

The test was played in Soweto, on the outskirts of Johannesburg, at the massive FNB Stadium. A month earlier the 95,000-capacity venue had hosted the final of the 2010 FIFA World Cup between the Netherlands and Spain. The All Blacks knew the Springboks were not wanting to find themselves as they had the previous year, suffering three straight losses to their fierce rivals. They were expecting a backlash from the 'Boks and from individual players who had not given their best performances while in

New Zealand. Among them, number eight Pierre Spies.

'I don't think [Spies] played as well as he would have liked in New Zealand,' Read told *Herald* rugby writer Gregor Paul. 'They are going to come at us and they are going to be determined to be a lot more accurate. But I don't think they can get too caught up in targeting individual players. I think it was our game plan that rocked them and we have to get that right again.'

The Africans made a key change to their loose trio, dropping Louw and bringing in Juan Smith, who made his side more competitive at the breakdown, allowing Spies to roam with ball in hand a bit more.

The Springboks led 16–14 at half-time and were still ahead 22–17 with just three minutes left on the clock. Then McCaw had an anxious wait while the TMO confirmed he had scored a try in the corner. The scores were tied! Carter had the side-line conversion to take the All Blacks into the lead by two points. It narrowly missed.

Referee Nigel Owens ruled there was still time to play.

Springbok captain Jean de Villiers, playing his 100th test for his country, admitted after the game that the South Africans were looking for field position from the kick-off so first-five Morne Steyn could have a dropped-goal attempt. But as they crabbed for field position, they turned the ball over …

The All Blacks counterattacked without hesitation. Nonu made a break in midfield, through the attempted tackle of de Villiers who lay devastated on the ground watching as Nonu threw a long pass to his left, where Dagg swooped and raced to the try line. In his delight, Dagg put a few hearts in mouths as he dived and grounded the ball perilously close to the dead ball line. (Henry later had a quiet word in his ear about not doing that again!) Carter converted. The All Blacks had won with a stunning finish 29–22.

This was the All Blacks' first win in Johannesburg since 1997.

McCaw acknowledged the play of his own team after the game and offered some sympathy to de Villiers, whose celebration had turned to custard:

> 'I'm happy we won but I feel sorry for Jean. For a guy like that he probably deserved better, but that's the way rugby goes. It's a cruel game.'

The final game for the All Blacks was against Australia in front of 80,000 people at ANZ Stadium in Sydney, a match in which McCaw led the side for the 52nd time in tests, breaking Sean Fitzpatrick's record.

Australia was doing its best to make sure it wasn't a memorable night for McCaw and, early in the second half, was ahead by 19–6. With 15 minutes to play, the Wallabies were up by 22–9. Then Read and McCaw combined from the back of a scrum close to the line. Read picked up the ball and ran wide to his left before popping an in-pass to McCaw, who crossed the line without a hand being laid on him. It was a lovely set-piece move, although there was some contention from Australian supporters that McCaw had detached early from the scrum.

The All Blacks still needed a converted try to win the game and this came when Read crashed over under the posts after the All Blacks had been on attack for a long period. Weepu converted. New Zealand 23, Australia 22. The men in black finished the Tri-Nations as the first team to remain unbeaten over their six matches, and set new records for most tries and most points (184).

Great Kieran Read All Blacks Moments #1

Test 26
New Zealand versus Australia 23–22
Sydney, Australia
10 September 2010

With less than eight minutes left on the clock in the 2010 Tri-Nations match against Australia, the All Blacks were behind by 16–22. As the All Black forwards attacked the line, the Australian defence held strong until … from a ruck right on the line, McCaw passed left to Read who was standing in line with the middle of the posts. Read ran on an angle back towards the right-hand upright where three Wallaby defenders stood. They were flat-footed, but *nothing* would have been able to stop Read from that close to the line. The try, converted by Weepu, clinched the game for the All Blacks.

Once again, the start of the end-of-year northern tour was a stopover in Hong Kong and a date with the Wallabies. Though Robbie Deans had begun his time in charge of the men in gold with an emphatic win, this had been the only one. The All Blacks had won the next 10 encounters between the two sides and were also sitting on an unbeaten 15-match streak. If they could beat the Aussies, the five matches on the tour itinerary gave them the chance to set a new world record for consecutive test wins.

In humid conditions, the All Blacks started the game slowly, conceding 12 unanswered points, but then scored 24 points themselves to lead 24–12 approaching the 60-minute mark. Australia scored a converted try to be only five points in

The Wallabies win in Hong Kong. Their wild celebrations would not be forgotten by the men in black.

arrears. All Black first-five Stephen Donald had what looked to be a well-placed penalty kick opportunity with a few minutes remaining to take the All Blacks to an eight-point lead. He missed it. Then with time up on the clock and the siren having sounded, Donald kicked for touch. But rather than kick short and safely for touch, the ball went long and missed touch. The Wallabies had their last chance to counterattack, and did so. The then wunderkind of Australian rugby, James O'Connor, scored in the corner — to bring the scores level — and then audaciously kicked the side-line conversion.

The Wallabies' ecstasy at having broken their 10-match losing streak was unfettered and their sledging, jubilant comments to members of the All Blacks could have made some of their cricketers blush! This Australian reaction to the win 26–24 would not be easily forgotten by the All Blacks.

The annoyed All Blacks then headed for Europe and gave Graham Henry his third Grand Slam as coach with wins against England (26–16), Scotland (49–3), Ireland (38–18) and

The young Wallabies star, James O'Connor.

Dan Carter, the highest points-scorer in test match history.

McCaw and Muliaina became the most-capped All Blacks in 2010.

Wales (37–25). Remarkably, the Irish victory was Henry's one hundredth as an international coach, while McCaw and Muliaina became the most-capped All Blacks of all time, overtaking Sean Fitzpatrick's record of 92.

Read was subbed off in the final match, against Wales, a game for which the All Blacks wore white armbands in remembrance of the 29 Pike River miners who had been killed in the West Coast coal mine explosion. Dan Carter overtook Jonny Wilkinson as the highest points-scorer in test match history.

Read suffered a leg injury just before half-time meaning that, for the first time in 11 matches,

he had not stayed on the field for the entire match. He had bagged three tries on tour, with one against England and a brace against Ireland.

The editors of the *Rugby Almanack of New Zealand* named him as one of their Five Players of the Year, a mere two years after they had named him one of the Promising Players of the Year. They wrote:

'In 2010 he confirmed that the number-eight position was his, and that any other occupant there would only be temporary … At season's end he was regarded as one of the premier

Anthony Boric, Sam Whitelock and Kieran Read all smiles after another win.

exponents of the craft worldwide. One hopes that the injury that took him from the field in the last game against Wales has no lasting effects … With his captain, they were the only two All Blacks to start in every test match this year. It is easy to agree with the word going around that he is a future All Black captain.'

At the national rugby awards held in Auckland in the middle of December, Read was crowned the New Zealand Player of the Year, winning the Kelvin R Tremain Memorial Trophy over fellow nominees McCaw and Brad Thorn. He had also

been nominated in the Super 14 Player of the Year category (which was won by Blues halfback Alby Mathewson). The top award was named after Tremain who was a standout loose forward for the All Blacks from 1959 to 1968. He played 86 games, including 38 tests and, for a time, held the record for most test tries (nine) by an All Black forward. In all, he played 268 first-class games of rugby and scored an amazing 136 tries. For a number of years, this was the second-most number of career tries scored by a New Zealand rugby player, but the most by a forward. It was 22 years before that number was overtaken by another dominant and gifted forward, Zinzan Brooke. When his playing days ended, Tremain became a noted administrator, and the rugby world was deeply saddened by his death in 1992 after a short illness. He was only 54 years old and the NZRU saw fit to memorialise his contribution to the national game by naming its highest player award after him.

When the award nominees were announced towards the end of November, *Herald* rugby writer Wynne Gray picked Read to receive the top accolade. 'This bloke is a machine without an off button', he wrote.

> 'Read has moved through this year with the authority of someone who is top of the world heap. His handling has been secure, his decisions from the base of the scrum have been crisp and strong, his power running a concern for defences while his defence has always been a strength … Tack on Read's ability as a lineout forward, at the tail or front, and his growing leadership authority, and it is easy to see how he has become such a core component of the All Blacks. There are murmurings about him as an All Black captain-in-waiting. Certainly, if he carries on with his current form, his name will be in the mix when McCaw calls it quits.'

Read had another new title not long after putting his rugby kit bag in storage (for a few weeks) at the end of the season. He became a father for the first time, to daughter Elle.

Earthquake

In days gone by, on winter afternoons, rugby crowds in the main stand at Lancaster Park could look out over the terraces on the other side of the field, past the city skyline to the rising, snow-capped Southern Alps. A scenic attraction for tourists and winter playground for skiers, their beauty belies the fact that they have been formed by thousands of years of seismic activity. Two large tectonic plates — the Australian and Pacific — have been crashing against each other, causing the uplift that is the mountainous spine that runs almost the length of the South Island.

Residents of Christchurch were used to occasional short tremors moving the earth with the motion of a slow wave. Every now and then the city would experience a sharper jolt. Most thought nothing of it. It was a part of living in New Zealand and it wasn't something peculiar to Christchurch alone.

When a magnitude 7.1 quake struck the city, though, at 4.35 a.m. on Saturday, 4 September 2010, it terrified the people of Christchurch and surrounding districts. Read and wife Bridget, who at the time was six months pregnant with Elle, cowered together under a door frame.

The rest of the country woke to news bulletins of the quake, and the media spent the day covering the story. Talkback radio was full of the tired voices of Cantabrians who were telling of their experience of the quake and reporting damage that daylight had revealed. Scientists scrambled to the site of the fault, in the countryside west of Christchurch, near Darfield.

The beautiful Garden City was visibly scarred by large fissures that had opened in the ground, by damage to buildings that had had their contents thrown about by the forces of the earth, and by the eerie pooling of liquefaction.

Miraculously, while there had been injuries, not one life had been lost. As repairs were undertaken across the region and aftershocks began to lessen in frequency and intensity, the hope was that quake had been 'the big one' and all would return to normal.

In an almost unprecedented seismic event, the quake of September 2010 proved to be merely the precursor to one of New Zealand's most devastating natural disasters.

Five months later, on 22 February 2011, another quake hit. At 12.51 p.m. Not miles from the city. It struck only 10 kilometres southeast of Christchurch city with a magnitude of 6.3. Not while most people were asleep. At lunchtime. It lasted only 10 seconds but the results were catastrophic: 183 people were killed.

As a result of the 2011 earthquake, the Crusaders played 17 games 'on the road', clocking up an estimated 100,000 kilometres of travel. Despite such demands, they remained positive, playing for the people of Canterbury.

Read was having a sushi lunch with McCaw at the Merivale Mall, just a few minutes' drive from the Crusaders' training base of Rugby Park. Overcrowded and disrupted mobile phone networks meant he couldn't initially contact wife Bridget. What was normally a short drive home from the mall to his Shirley home turned into a 20-minute ordeal as Read manoeuvred his car through the damaged streets, all thoughts on the safety of his family. 'I wasn't immediately sure how big the earthquake was,' he told the *New Zealand Herald*'s James Ihaka. 'It was not until I saw how much damage there was that I realised there was a lot of danger. I just hoped my family was at home. My wife and baby were there, thankfully, and they were pretty shaken up. Our backyard was filling up with silt.'

The Reads had to relocate for a time, due to the lack of power and water.

In the days after the earthquake, the Crusaders' match against the Hurricanes was rightly cancelled (declared a draw and points shared). Members of the Crusaders squad appeared with shovels, gumboots and wheelbarrows to help residents of the eastern suburbs clear their properties of liquefaction.

Read told Ihaka:

> 'This is a bigger thing than footy at the moment; it was the only way to go for us, to be honest. We're just wanting to help out in our community, and are doing whatever we can. It's just a few of the boys … we've just been digging and loading wheelbarrows, heaps of them.'

Damage to the home of Canterbury rugby and cricket, AMI Stadium, was assessed. It was a write-off. Large cracks ran through the relatively new Deans Stand. The Crusaders team was now homeless. Upcoming Rugby World Cup matches would have to be reallocated to other centres.

In the three months after the quake, the Crusaders played 17 games, all of which were 'on the road'. Their home ground became Nelson's Trafalgar Park, where they played four matches. Timaru, also within the franchise catchment, hosted two games. The run of venues was Nelson, Nelson, Dunedin, London, Timaru, Mt Maunganui, Nelson, Perth, Cape Town, Bloemfontein, Napier, Brisbane, Timaru and Wellington.

The Napier game was also considered a 'home' fixture, as was the match at Twickenham in London against the Sharks. This had been arranged largely as a fundraiser, given that the Crusaders were losing revenue by not having crowds at home games in Christchurch.

Remarkably, for all the travel and the turmoil in Christchurch, the side made the final against the Reds in Brisbane following a resounding 36–8 win over the Sharks in their quarterfinal and then a semifinal win, 29–10, over the Sharks in Cape Town.

The two sides had met six weeks earlier with the Reds snatching a 17–16 win, thanks to a controversial late penalty awarded against Richie McCaw by referee Stu Dickinson and kicked by Quade Cooper. Since then, the Reds had enjoyed one weekend without a match while the Crusaders kept packing and unpacking their bags around South Africa and New Zealand on their way to a 10th Super Rugby final.

President of the Canterbury Rugby Supporters' Club and tireless advocate of sport in the region, Dick Tayler (himself a sporting legend as a result of his 1974 Commonwealth Games gold medal in the 10,000 metres), spoke for all the Crusaders fans when he told the *Herald*'s Paul Harper:

'Everyone is just so excited the Crusaders have done so well this year, particularly not having had home games as such. The success of the Crusaders has really given people a big boost. We all salute the team and the squad. Of course, you've also got to remember their wives, partners and families back home — their support crew — it's been hard on them as well.'

Richie McCaw, who had an abbreviated series of only six appearances due to an ongoing foot injury, tried to brush away praise for the team's efforts in reaching the final, as well as concerns about what toll it might take in the final that would undoubtedly be an emotional one for them. He told the *Herald*'s Dylan Cleaver:

'You get a choice, don't you? Use it as an excuse and everyone will probably pat you on the back and say, "Oh well, that's fair enough." We made a decision when all the carnage happened at home that we would stand up for the people at home and for what the Crusaders mean. We have given ourselves a chance now.'

An Australian Super Rugby record crowd of 52,113 packed the stands of Suncorp Stadium for the final. The Crusaders, wearing their alternate strip of grey with red left shoulder and sleeve, led by 7–6 at half-time thanks to a Dan Carter special: a right-footed grubber kick and gather from inside the Reds' 22-metre line. The scores were tied 13–13 into the last 15 minutes until a piece of magic by Reds halfback, Will Genia, secured a first Super Rugby title for the home side.

From a ruck centre-field on the Reds' 10-metre line, Genia, after looking as though he was thinking of lobbing a kick in behind the Crusaders' defensive line, ran straight between two defenders … and ran … and ran … and scored. It was noticeably deflating for the Crusaders and, suddenly, the campaign that had taken them over an estimated 100,000 km looked to have taken its toll. The team that had so valiantly carried on after an earthquake had destroyed their homes and stadium, and that hoped their efforts would give some cheer to the people of Christchurch, suddenly looked exhausted, mentally and physically.

Corey Flynn explained to media just what effect the travel demands had had on the families of those involved with the Crusaders:

> 'The wives and partners and kids of some of the boys were fair fed up with it, and understandably because while it was hard getting up and going every week, it was also easy because we were staying at nice hotels and the ground wasn't shaking. We were safe, it was the families back here … at any point there could have been a massive earthquake and we didn't know what was going to happen.'

With their 'around the world in 18 games' campaign over, Read, who had played in 16 of the matches, admitted to *New Idea* magazine that the constantly revolving doors of airports and hotels — on top of post-quake emotions — did have an effect on players:

> 'It just backs up on you. For a few weeks you could do it, but as the season wore on it became more difficult leaving people at home who were still going through quite a tough time.'

The players' efforts were recognised, not just by local fans or those interested in Super Rugby. They were nominated for one of the Laureus World Sports Awards, in the category of Comeback of the Year.

The day after the final, Read, a newly appointed ambassador for the Yellow-Eyed Penguin Trust New Zealand, was named in the All Blacks squad for an abbreviated Tri-Nations series and match against Fiji prior to the Rugby World Cup beginning in September.

He later offered a somewhat philosophical comment about the personal effect of the Christchurch disaster on him. 'I think my whole approach to life is about enjoyment and making the most of what you have now,' he told *New Idea* magazine. 'I don't know whether that's a change resulting from the earthquake or starting a family — because Elle came along just before the earthquake — but with the earthquake, you just don't know what could happen.'

Rugby World Cup 2011

The Crusaders' All Black players had to put the disappointment of the final loss to the Reds (and the accumulated fatigue) quickly behind them and change their focus to a shortened Tri-Nations series, with the three sides playing each other only twice. During the tournament the squads for the looming Rugby World Cup had to be named. This was a somewhat uncomfortable arrangement for the All Blacks and the Wallabies, who wanted to delay the naming of their respective squads until after their final Tri-Nations match. Instead, the powers-that-be decreed that the announcements should be four days before the test.

All Black assistant coach Steve Hansen, who knew all about dealing with the daily effects of post-quake Canterbury, told media:

> *'Invariably, what happens after something like that, combined with the emotional toll that they've gone through and all the travel, is that there'll be a big sigh and a tired period will come in. We'll look at and try and map out a programme that allows them to freshen up both physically and mentally and be able to peak at the right time.'*

The first thing to do was to make sure the Bledisloe Cup was put back in the cupboard for another year, and this was duly done with a resounding 30–14 win over the Wallabies (who had lost to Samoa 22–32 three weeks earlier) at Eden Park.

With that coveted trophy secure, Read and other Crusaders players, such as McCaw, Thorn and Carter, weren't with the All Blacks when they boarded a plane bound for South Africa to play the Springboks in Port Elizabeth. The All Blacks scored the only try of the match, to Richard Kahui, but Morne Steyn kicked five penalties and a dropped goal to win the match by 18–5.

Henry selected a first-string side for the final Tri-Nations match against Australia in Brisbane. The Wallabies had the possibility of winning the title for the first time since 2001 if they could defeat the All Blacks. This they did, on the back of a first half that saw them lead 20–3. The first 40 minutes saw the departure from the field of a hobbling Read, the All Blacks made a dozen or

Read was so integral to the All Blacks' 2011 Rugby World Cup campaign, the selectors were prepared to start the tournament without him.

more errors, and a storming run to the try line by the ageless Fijian giant wing-turned number eight Radike Samo left men in black jerseys sprawling across the turf.

The half-time deficit was the greatest the All Blacks had conceded in test history but by the 59th minute they had levelled the scores, thanks to tries by the old midfield mates Conrad Smith and Nonu. But another fairytale finish for the All Blacks was not to be. Kurtley Beale scored for the Wallabies, ensuring they held on for a 25–20 win.

Henry told media the following day that he and his fellow coaches thought the plan to rest players for the South African game and then change the line-up in Brisbane was 'the best step going forward into the Rugby World Cup,

and it didn't gel for some reason or other. It just didn't gel.' He was also quick to warn Australia that Tri-Nations success was no guarantee of World Cup success.

Every World Cup year, rugby fans hold their breath that no squad member will suffer injuries that could keep them out of the tournament. In 2011, All Black fans tensed up during the Super 14 and Tri-Nations competitions any time a frontline player was slow to get up off the ground, hobbled towards the side-line or grabbed at the back of their thigh.

Richie McCaw was making light of a niggling stress fracture that had seen a screw inserted into the fifth metatarsal bone in his right foot. This caused him to miss the first two months of Super Rugby, while one or two of the more opinionated sports journalists were declaring that his days as an All Black were over.

So when Kieran Read damaged his ankle 12 minutes into the Brisbane test, a cloud of doom began to descend on some fans, fearing that 2011 could be like the five previous World Cups when the All Blacks failed to win 'Bill' — the William Webb Ellis trophy. Adding to the growing tension was the fact that for the first time since 1987 — the inaugural tournament won by New Zealand — the cup was being held in 'our backyard'. The All Blacks were expected to win. Nothing else would satisfy the public.

As Read made his way from the field, gingerly putting pressure on his ankle, every armchair doctor diagnosed the worst — he wouldn't make the World Cup. After all, his fellow Crusader, lock Sam Whitelock, had suffered the same sort of injury earlier in the year and been on the side-line for over two months. If Read's high ankle sprain was as severe as that, he could likely miss the entire World Cup campaign.

The diagnosis from All Blacks doctor Deb Robinson was that:

> 'Kieran has torn the ligament between the tibia and fibula at the front of his left ankle and, while it's still early days in his recovery, with aggressive rehabilitation we are aiming to have him available to play near the end of the [World Cup] round robin.'

While the comment was specific in terms of the nature of the injury, there was still enough vagueness for fans to keep fretting: 'still early days', 'with aggressive rehabilitation', 'aiming to', 'near the end of the round robin'. So Rugby World Cup 2011 began without one of the All Blacks' form players, who had also missed the warm-up test against Fiji in Dunedin, an earthquake

fundraiser for Christchurch charities KidsCan and Plunket, that the NZRU supported.

New Zealand All Blacks Rugby World Cup Squad 2011

Corey Flynn (Canterbury)
Andrew Hore (Taranaki)
Keven Mealamu (Auckland)
John Afoa (Auckland)
Ben Franks (Tasman)
Owen Franks (Canterbury)
Tony Woodcock (North Harbour)
Anthony Boric (North Harbour)
Brad Thorn (Canterbury)
Sam Whitelock (Canterbury)
Ali Williams (Auckland)
Jerome Kaino (Auckland)
Richie McCaw (Canterbury)
Kieran Read (Canterbury)
Adam Thomson (Otago)
Victor Vito (Wellington)
Jimmy Cowan (Southland)
Andy Ellis (Canterbury)
Piri Weepu (Wellington)
Daniel Carter* (Canterbury)
Colin Slade** (Canterbury)
Richard Kahui (Waikato)
Ma'a Nonu (Wellington)
Conrad Smith (Wellington)
Sonny Bill Williams (Canterbury)
Israel Dagg (Hawke's Bay)
Zac Guildford (Hawke's Bay)
Cory Jane (Wellington)
Mils Muliaina (Waikato)
Isaia Toeava (Auckland)

*replaced by Aaron Cruden (Manawatu)
**replaced by Stephen Donald (Waikato)

The tournament got under way on 9 September, with a dazzling opening ceremony at Eden Park, followed by the All Blacks resisting a concerted challenge from Pacific neighbours, Tonga, winning the first game 41–10. It was the smallest losing margin for the Tongan 'Ikale Tahi' (Sea Eagles) against the All Blacks, which led to some media grumbling that the All Blacks had not played well. Read's stand-in, Victor Vito, was widely criticised for what some saw as a lacklustre performance.

The next match in Hamilton on 16 September was against Japan, who, like Tonga, also have the national colours of red and white. Having never had the All Blacks score less than 74 points against them in the four previous games the teams had played, the 'Brave Blossoms' were not expected to pose too great a threat to the All Blacks. Under the guidance of coach John Kirwan they were playing a fast game, but a lack of size in the forwards was expected to be their undoing against the big, mobile All Blacks.

So it proved to be. The All Blacks won by 83–7, although a huge cheer sounded when Japanese winger Hirotoki Onozawa sprinted away for an intercept try.

While in Hamilton, reporter David Long spoke to Read about his injured ankle, rehabilitation and the dangers of not being available to play.

'I'm out of the moon boot so from today I can actually get round and walk about on it a bit normally. It's feeling really good and all signs are on track to hopefully be back for the Canada game, the last pool game. Hopefully, I'll be running again next week — that's the plan at this stage. I've been into the pool and doing a lot of rehab with it, so it's feeling good …'

Tongan players and fans brought great passion to the 2011 Rugby World Cup, making them worthy opponents in the opening game of the tournament against the All Blacks.

Victor Vito (above) deputised for Read in the match against Tonga, while the game against Japan (below) was a fast-paced try-scoring fiesta.

'You don't want to be letting other people have opportunities in your position,' he continued.

> *'I'm helping them as much as I can and as a team we want to be moving forward, but in the back of my mind I want to get out on the field again as soon as I can … I can bike, so my aerobic fitness should still be fairly strong: I suppose it's going to be match fitness which might be lacking. It always is when you come back from injury, but I'll definitely give it my all when I get out there.'*

The next day, Read and the All Blacks flew down to Christchurch to spend four days training and meeting the public in the city that had been deprived of All Black games by the quake.

A week later, the All Blacks were back at Eden Park to face France in a clash that would decide who qualified as the top team from Pool A. The French were well-known for their ability to disrupt All Black World Cup campaigns. Their semifinal win in 1999 and quarterfinal triumph in 2007 were deeply ingrained in the memories of All Blacks fans. Fans and media wondered aloud whether they would spoil the All Blacks' party in this game. After all, they were the last team to beat the All Blacks on Eden Park, albeit way back in 1994.

The answer was an emphatic no. With Richie McCaw playing his 100th test, the All Blacks won 37–17. The win was so definitive — five tries to two — questions were asked of the French. Were they just foxing, knowing that a loss to the All Blacks would move them across to the other side of the tournament draw, therefore giving them a potentially safer road to a final against … the All Blacks?

Under tireless, clinical captain Thierry Dusautoir, one of the world's best loose forwards, such thinking was an insult and it earned the ire of coach Marc Lièvremont. But the loss and the reaction to the French performance would stoke the fire of French motivation later in the tournament.

The All Blacks' final pool match was against Canada — the Canucks — at Westpac Stadium in Wellington on 2 October (another team with colours of red and white!).

There had been surprises aplenty the day before. Tonga had beaten France at the same venue 19–14, their pack valiantly outplaying the French and seeming to get stronger as the game went on, and thoughts of a famous upset became a reality.

But this was not the major rugby headline that night. Local evening news programmes led with the story that Dan Carter had torn the abductor muscle at the top of his left leg and would be out for … *the rest of the tournament!* Footage of Carter at training making a seemingly innocuous kick and then slumping to the ground before bravely, but in noticeable discomfort, making his way from the ground were played and replayed. The emotional rollercoaster All Blacks fans were on took a sudden dive downwards.

But there was also some good news in the All Blacks' final pool game — Kieran Read was back, running on with the team for the first time in the tournament. Those who weren't previously aware of what had prevented him playing the previous three games could quite easily see why when after only a few minutes of the game his left boot and sock were covered in a thick wrap of white tape.

When asked by reporters if he had been worried about the chances of further damaging his ankle he replied:

> *'You have just got to get any of those thoughts out of your mind. When you cross the field you just have to think about what you've got to do.'*

While it was a relief to see Read back on deck, most eyes were on the performance of Colin Slade, Carter's deputy, who looked most assured in poor weather against a passionate Canadian team. Truly eye-catching were four blistering tries scored by wing Zac Guildford and the imposing, physical display of Jerome Kaino, who scored two tries himself and made players he'd tackled feel as if they'd just run into a tree trunk. A number of times the Canadians helplessly tried to bring him to the ground while his legs pumped hard and, with head down, he relentlessly drove on for metre after metre. Amid all this, and a win by 79 to 15, Read played 50 minutes without any recurrence of his ankle injury.

What a week to be an All Black fan!

The All Blacks had topped Pool A, winning four from four, scoring 240 points and conceding only 49. Their next opponent would be Argentina, who had come second in Pool B.

In the preceding quarterfinals, France beat England 19–12 and Australia defeated South Africa 11–9 (in a match that saw referee Bryce Lawrence become public enemy number one for South African fans).

The All Blacks went back to Eden Park for what some expected would be an easy win over the Pumas, a game that would be fullback Mils Muliaina's 100th test.

All did not go to plan and when Argentina was in front by one point, 7–6, after half an hour, the ghost of the All Blacks' quarterfinal loss

Midfield bursts from Nonu and Williams in the quarterfinal against Argentina. Try as they did, it was Read and Brad Thorn (from a Read pass) who scored the two vital tries.

Former All Blacks captain and NZRU chairman Jock Hobbs was terminally ill when he presented Muliaina with his 100th test cap after the quarterfinal against Argentina.

at Cardiff four years earlier was looming. Two minutes later, Colin Slade's tournament was over when he suffered a groin injury just like Carter. Unbelievable!

Aaron Cruden, who hadn't been part of the original squad, took the field as Slade's replacement but Piri Weepu had taken over the kicking duties when Carter limped out of the tournament. He set a new All Black record for penalty goals in a World Cup with seven successful kicks.

Read thought he had scored the first All Black try of the night, only for it to be disallowed by the TMO. Finally, in the 67th minute, he dived across the line in the left-hand corner for a try that finally saw the Pumas wilt and the All Blacks win 33–10.

The Argentinians had played with their typical robustness in the forwards, muscling into their work at the scrum, maul and breakdown. For Read, it was the perfect outing to physically prepare for the match the following week: a semifinal against Australia at Eden Park on 16 October.

It was a nervous week for supporters as they pondered the potential the Wallabies had to end the All Blacks' World Cup dream. They had twice beaten the All Blacks in semifinals before, in 1991 and 2003. They had also beaten the All Blacks 25–20 in their last encounter to clinch the Tri-Nations title. But the All Blacks privately delighted in hearing the news that the Wallabies would be their next opponent, and training sessions during the week reflected a noticeable lift in intensity.

Jerome Kaino told the *Herald*'s veteran rugby reporter Wynne Gray that the Brisbane loss was being used as a source of motivation for the team:

> 'If we win the physical battle, it goes a long way towards winning the contest. Nothing changes; we just have to meet the intensity that semifinal rugby brings … The guys definitely want to improve after that performance and I'm sure the guys wanted another game to build into the World Cup after that performance, but it wasn't to be. We're looking forward to seeing them again. We see them as our number one foe.'

Read also spoke to media in the run-up to the match and pointed to the battle of the loose forwards.

> 'That is an area where we see we can [dominate] and, especially in that breakdown area, we back ourselves. You know, it is a good challenge because David Pocock played really well last week. He is one of the form number sevens in the competition, so it is a great challenge and we back ourselves because we always do when we run out there with the black jersey on. The rivalry between Australia and New Zealand is something we expect to win and want to win every time. That is pretty straightforward so from that point of view, it is something you want to do every time you play them.'

Much media attention was focused on Wallabies number 10, Quade Cooper, whose cheap shots against McCaw in the recent Hong Kong and Brisbane tests — including a knee to the head of the All Blacks skipper — had not been forgotten. Rather, they were being replayed on television and mentioned incessantly. Rugby scribes speculated on which Cooper would turn up to play on the night: the irrepressible, skilled game-breaker, or the hapless man caught in the headlights. It turned out to be the latter.

Cooper put the opening kick-off out on the full, to delighted hoots and jeers from All Blacks fans. He made poor passes, dropped high balls kicked his way, and kicked poorly. He also felt the ferocity of the All Blacks' tackling, as did most of his teammates. So poor was his play, the BBC's Tom Fordyce coined a new dictionary definition:

> **Quade** 1. (v): to crumble under pressure; 'He lost his job after quadeing badly.'
> 2. (n): the act of messing something up; 'I made a right quade of that raspberry pavlova.'

Quade Cooper's semifinal got off to the worst possible start.

Jerome Kaino demonstrates the defensive power that typified his and the All Blacks' play during the 2011 Rugby World Cup.

Dagg was in scintillating form during the 2011 Rugby World Cup, as exemplified by the pass he threw while airborne for Nonu to score the only try of the semifinal versus Australia.

The men in black rampaged over their nearest rivals to win 20–6. Read was all smiles at the end of the game, having played with great physicality himself as part of a scrum that demolished the Wallabies at that set piece and as a defender who stopped ball runners in their tracks, no doubt leaving them feeling the impact of his big shoulders for days afterwards.

It was a sensational performance by the men in black, particularly by wing Cory Jane, who was named Man of the Match. So impressed was coach Henry with the way his team had played in such a crucial game, he was quick to label it the best by any of his teams during his eight-year tenure.

The unforgiving Eden Park crowd chanted 'Four more years, boys. Four more years!' at the Wallabies, harking back to the famous sledge from George Gregan during the 2003 World Cup semifinal, lost by the All Blacks 10–22.

With the Wallabies dispatched, there was another week of preparation before the All Blacks faced France in the World Cup final at Eden Park. The Tricolores had won their semifinal against Wales somewhat controversially. The 9–8 result was secured against 14 men after inspirational Welsh captain Sam Warburton was sent off in the 14th minute by referee Alain Rolland, following what was deemed to be a dangerous spear tackle.

In the week before the final, local media trumpeted that the result was a foregone

In their 2011 Rugby World Cup semifinal, the Wallabies had little answer to the All Blacks' pace and power, on attack and defence.

conclusion. The All Blacks would win easily over a French side they had conquered in pool play — a team which had struggled to beat a Welsh team that had one fewer player on the field for most of the match.

Such hometown arrogance simply added to the motivation for the French who wanted to become only the second team from the northern hemisphere, after England, to win the gold trophy.

Some commentators were expressing concern that given the way the All Blacks had physically intimidated and demolished Australia the week before, they had, in essence, played their final a week early and that their bodies would still be feeling the effects of that match.

Graham Henry told allblacks.com:

'This is the biggest game of the players' lives and there is obvious excitement and anticipation at what lies ahead. To be playing in the final of the Rugby World Cup in front of our home crowd is going to be massive and a very special occasion for the team as well as our fans. The support the team has received from New Zealanders throughout the tournament has been incredibly humbling and we know the country will be right behind us on Sunday night.'

There were new milestones being achieved by players that were easy to overlook in the excitement of the week. McCaw, Read and

Kaino became the most-capped loose forward trio in All Black history. Their 21st appearance together saw them take the record previously held by McCaw, Rodney So'oialo and Wellington hardman Jerry Collins. Mealamu was also equalling Sean Fitzpatrick's record of 92 caps for an All Black hooker.

Since the inception of the Rugby World Cup, the final matches have developed a reputation of being somewhat dour, low-scoring affairs. With the exception of when New Zealand beat France in the 1987 final 29–9, and when the Wallabies won their second crown in 1999

against the same opponent 35–12, the greatest winning margin had been nine points. In 1991, Australia defeated England 12–6. Four years later, the Springboks beat the All Blacks when Joel Stransky kicked a dropped goal in extra time for the team from the Rainbow Nation to win 15–12. The 2003 final went to extra time, with a Jonny Wilkinson dropped goal securing the win for England 20–17. South Africa won its second title by beating England 15–6 in 2007, all points being scored from the boot — seven penalty goals! As for tries, they were a rarity. Hopes were high that the 2011 final would be a great spectacle of running rugby from two of the best proponents of this kind of game.

However, in the event, the game could not have been any more different from what had been predicted.

Dusautoir's French team, wearing white jerseys, showed that they would be no walkover from the moment they lined up in a V formation with arms linked to accept the All Blacks' haka. Their steely stares were unbroken as the All Blacks delivered a pulsating challenge.

Early in the match, Read made space for wing Richard Kahui and took the ball up in midfield to get the All Blacks over the advantage line, but, as the game became tighter and more tense, he showed his value in the more traditional role of a number eight, contesting rucks and mauls, never shirking tackles and winning vital lineout ball.

At the half-time break the score was only 5–0 to the All Blacks, thanks to a well-taken lineout move that saw prop Tony Woodcock crash over the line.

Read later told media:

> 'At half-time I was the most nervous I had ever been. I certainly felt it could have swung either way. I didn't know what the referee was going to do but I

Tony Woodcock, try-scoring hero for the All Blacks in the 2011 Rugby World Cup final.

had faith in what we were doing. As a forward, we wanted to take control and just see out the game really.'

Only minutes into the second half, Stephen Donald (who had become the All Blacks' fourth first-five of the tournament after Cruden left the field injured, and was on the field wearing a jersey several sizes too small) kicked a penalty to take the All Blacks out to 8–0. Shortly afterwards, French captain Dusautoir scored by the posts and the conversion cut the All Blacks' lead to one point.

Now the game became really tense for all concerned.

In a rather revealing statement, Cory Jane later told Gregor Paul that the frazzled nerves were not limited to those off the field. The All Blacks were starting to feel the pressure that was beyond anything most of them had experienced before. The unity that had been a key component to their campaign was being tested in the white-hot intensity of the World Cup final.

'I started to think that after having done so much that we were starting to play absolutely terribly. A few boys started abusing each other. If someone dropped it, instead of doing what we had been doing in the past, words would be exchanged. Some guys started not telling the other guys the moves.'

All Black depth was both tested and proven when Stephen Donald became the fourth number 10 used by the team in the 2011 Rugby World Cup.

Kaino tries to make ground against the resolute French in the 2011 Rugby World Cup.

As All Blacks fans' blood pressure rose and fingernails were gnawed during the nerve-wracking final 20 minutes, Read, McCaw and Kaino seemed inseparable as they defended drives by the French forwards, or prudently attacked French ball at the breakdown. The almost ashen-faced Graham Henry watched on anxiously as turnovers were made at crucial times with play crabbing about the field. Crucially, the All Blacks didn't concede a penalty. Henry later admitted that a brief period in the second half was the most nervous he had been through the cup campaign and he had started wondering how his family, particularly, would be able to handle the

public reaction if the All Blacks lost.

As the clock ticked closer to fulltime, there seemed to be no way for the All Blacks to wrest the ball from the possession of the French. Then a mistake came. Not from the All Blacks, but from French replacement Jean-Marc Doussain, who had only just come on to the field. He knocked the ball on. Finally, the All Blacks had the chance to control the ball, but, more crucially, they had a scrum, the setting of which could eat up some valuable seconds, which seemed to be ticking as slowly as minutes, or even hours, to the most nervous of All Blacks fans.

The scrum was won by the All Blacks and

The All Blacks are world champions for the second time, while the French are left as runners-up for the third time.

then the forwards took the ball for a series of 'pick and go' moves from the back of rucks. The clock kept ticking down. At last, the final hooter sounded and halfback Andy Ellis booted the ball into the ecstatic crowd jumping up and down in the ASB stand.

The All Blacks had won 8–7! They would finally have their name on the Webb Ellis trophy for a second time.

With more relief than jubilation, McCaw slowly rose from the turf to be embraced by his teammates. The cheers and applause from the crowd rolled on and on with few leaving the stadium. All Blacks supporters, like the players themselves, were giddy with delight. Rugby writers filed their match reports, many acclaiming it as the best final yet.

When McCaw finally left the field for the changing rooms, World Cup winner's medal around his neck, he then removed his right boot, and all who saw his foot were astounded at just how swollen it was. Read was full of praise for his skipper after the match.

'He was great. He had spent a lot of time preparing for that moment, for that pressure. It was awesome and immense, and to even be on the field and playing so well with that injury was incredible.'

Great Kieran Read All Blacks Moments #2

Test 37
2011 Rugby World Cup Final
New Zealand versus France
Eden Park, Auckland
23 October 2011
8–7

Rugby World Cup finals are usually dour, tight contests that see forward packs in tight tussles, spending much of their time with their heads in rucks or mauls. The 2011 final when the All Blacks met France at Eden Park was no different, with both teams knowing that the slightest mistake could offer the other side a match-winning chance. So in a game that offered Read few of the open running opportunities he thrived on, he undertook his core roles almost faultlessly. He led the number of metres gained by the All Black forwards and won all seven of the lineout throws to him. This was half the team total, showing off another of his skills that has added to the variety the All Blacks can use at set pieces.

On his return to Christchurch, where the players were publicly congratulated at a function in Hagley Park (after having been paraded up Auckland's Queen Street in front of cheering crowds estimated by some to have been close to 200,000 in number), Read told reporter Patrick McKendry:

'Just seeing the boys, and being around them, that's what makes you emotional, and so much has gone on. I don't think we could have not won, it just wouldn't have been right. It was pretty great for

us to get up and do it. For myself, you knew how much it meant to the country. Obviously, coming from Christchurch, how disappointed they've been, missing out and everything going on, so I suppose it was for the whole of New Zealand that drove you to succeed …
It's a great way to end the year. I'll never forget this year, it's been a hell of a ride.'

The final whistle at the World Cup brought to an end a number of All Black careers. Read had re-signed with the New Zealand Rugby Union during the year, but only for another season. While he had no intention of leaving the Crusaders, nor New Zealand, one matter that became important in negotiations was the impending introduction of the rugby players' Collective Bargaining Agreement.

This is an employment contract between individual players (as represented by the New Zealand Rugby Players' Association) and New Zealand Rugby. It replaced and improved on the previous agreement by including women's rugby and reducing the financial burden on struggling ITM Cup unions. Crucially, there were to be increased player payments and benefits. Players selected for the 2015 Rugby World Cup could expect to receive an additional $35,000 if the team made the final, and a further $115,000 if they won the tournament!

Hence the delay for Read in signing a new long-term contract with New Zealand Rugby. He told Christchurch rugby writer Richard Knowler that he was more than willing to keep playing rugby in New Zealand rather than look to go offshore and, in the process, have an OE with his family.

'I'm really keen. Really keen. It's something that will be worked out in due course. It is carrying on at the moment.'

Kaino and Read — world champions!

When the time came he re-signed, not just until the end of the new collective agreement (31 December 2015), but through until 2017. Read told a press conference he attended with Sam Whitelock, who was also extending his time with the NZRU, that:

> 'It's exciting news. This is the place where I want to be and I want to be playing my footy for the Crusaders and for the All Blacks. In some ways, I guess, the length of the contract was *the biggest decision and for my family it makes sense. Certainly, exciting times for me ahead here in New Zealand and really looking forward to that.'*

The end of the tournament also saw the end of Graham Henry's tenure as head coach. His eight seasons had been marked by having to deal with the fallout from the All Blacks' worst World Cup result, through to their best in 24 years. The team had played with attacking flair and marked defensive cohesion. His winning percentage stood at 85 per cent, with 88 wins from 103 tests. It was an unprecedented figure for the All Blacks in the professional era.

Wayne Smith also stepped down from the coaching panel to take up a position with the Chiefs Super Rugby franchise.

Given the success of the team at the cup, there seemed to be little discernible opposition to Steve Hansen's desire to step up from assistant to head coach. Following the process of the NZRU calling for applicants and conducting interviews, he was duly appointed in December 2011, along with assistants Ian Foster and Aussie McLean. Grant Fox joined the management team as a selector.

The challenge that had for so long seemed insurmountable — being world champions again — had been conquered. Now there were new goals. One of these was for Hansen to build the team and style of play over the next four years to successfully defend the Webb Ellis trophy in England in 2015. No side had yet won two cups in a row.

The All Black coaches knew that the team could not continue to use the same structures and systems on-field for another four years. They had to remain innovative and to keep surprising the chasing pack of opponents and their coaches, who were studying the All Blacks' every move. Hansen wanted his players to be able to pose a triple threat to opponents in being able to run, pass and kick.

'It comes with a huge amount of responsibility, and all I can say is that I'm passionate about rugby, passionate about New Zealand, passionate about the All Blacks jersey and its legacy, and I look forward to the next two years with this team and taking it forward and enhancing that legacy,' said Hansen. 'I'm a firm believer that when the All Blacks are at their best, they are using all fifteen players on the field, or playing at a pace of energy that other teams struggle to do and struggle to keep up with.'

Rugby Returns to Christchurch

On 23 March 2012, the Crusaders finally played a home game again in Christchurch. The new Addington Stadium had quickly been erected, in a little over three months, with a seating capacity of 17,500. The ground was very reminiscent of purpose-built football and rugby grounds in the northern hemisphere where, not having to accommodate cricket over in the summer months, the seating reaches in close to the playing field. While of course brand new, the stadium had features that linked it to rugby's past, both in Christchurch and around New Zealand's most famous venues. The big screen and goalposts were rescued from the irreparable AMI Stadium, along with turf that hadn't been a casualty of liquefaction. The lights came from Dunedin's legendary old home of rugby, Carisbrook. There were also contributions from the other end of the country, namely Eden Park (the steel) and Mt Smart Stadium (seating).

New Zealand rugby fans should also be aware that in the same way people around the country and the world donate money to earthquake appeals, the French and English rugby unions also made significant donations to the NZRU.

IRB member unions and RWC 2011 also donated almost half a million dollars to the Canterbury Rugby Earthquake Relief Charitable Trust.

Read told APNZ that the new venue, on the site of the old Rugby League Park, was:

> '… going to lift every player and the fans are going to love it. People are at the stage where they're over everything that's happened, and talking about it. We just want to move forward. Being back here for the first time is the first step forward for a lot of people, and I guess a bit of a release for others. The mood is pretty positive and it's time to get going again … At first fans weren't turning up for a variety of reasons, they were doing it tough, but there has been a switch, I guess, over the whole country in the last wee while. Coming back here with the Crusaders and being able to play on our own ground, and the work that we do in the community, has helped. The fans seem to appreciate that and come out to support us.'

Steve Hansen was appointed All Blacks coach after Graham Henry determined that the All Blacks would only get better.

The Crusaders had seven home games in the round robin, including three in a row at home against the Blues, the Highlanders and the Hurricanes. Then Super Rugby took a hiatus as the domestic test series began.

Steve Hansen's first test as head coach of the All Blacks came against Ireland at Eden Park on 9 June 2012. Jerome Kaino had departed New Zealand for a stint in Japan, leaving Victor Vito, Adam Thomson and Liam Messam to compete for the number six jersey. (It was one Messam made his own until Kaino returned in 2014 and was once again included in the All Blacks squad.)

For once, the All Blacks started their domestic season with a hiss and a roar. They looked sharp, refreshed and carried the confidence of being the new world champions. The backs were in stunning form and the Irish left Eden Park wondering just how they had been beaten so comprehensively, by 42 to 10.

Read's spectacular try-scoring near miss (see box opposite) had highlighted the All Blacks' attention to every facet of the game and the possibilities for possession to be gained from them. Prior to his departure, Kaino had told allblacks.com:

> 'We've also been working on our kick-offs quite a lot recently. It's like the third set piece, after scrums and lineouts. It's somewhere we can target to get hold of the ball and to make sure it's hard for the opposition to settle into the game.'

The following week in Christchurch, the first test in the city for two years was played in front of almost 21,000 fans. The Irish were a completely different team, determined to put on a better performance than they had seven days earlier. What a revelation they were! Their forwards were not going to be whipping boys for the second week in a row, and their backs

Great Kieran Read All Blacks Moments #3

Test 38
New Zealand versus Ireland, 42–10
Eden Park, Auckland
9 June 2012

Julian Savea had a dream debut scoring three tries, but one of the most remarkable events of the match was when Read almost scored one of the greatest individual tries ever seen. Ireland had scored a try in the 50th minute (to make the score 30–10 to the All Blacks). Carter restarted with a high drop-kick to his right, which was coming down just beyond the 10-metre line. Read chased the ball and leapt between three Irish players. Catching the ball in two hands, he then steamed over the 22 towards the Irish line and the right-hand corner. A desperate tackle from the Irish second-five brought Read to ground, but his momentum was still carrying him towards the line. As he reached out to place the ball, Irish captain Brian O'Driscoll slid in from the side to contest the ball. Referee Nigel Owens consulted the TMO and the decision was no try.

The effort of Read perfectly encapsulated his reading of a play, aerial ability and pace. He later told *The Press*'s Richard Knowler:

> '*It was one of those ones that is disappointing when you don't make it because no one remembers it now.*'

Oh, we remember it, all right!

played with better formation and handling. The same could not be said for their All Blacks counterparts, who had none of the lustre of the week before. Before you knew it, Ireland were leading 10–0.

Read was replaced by Sam Cane at half-time after suffering a knock to the head, with the Irish leading 10–9. The second half was taut and tense, and with the score at 19–19, Irish number 10 Johnny Sexton had a long-range penalty attempt to take the lead. This came from a high tackle by Israel Dagg, which saw him sent to the sin bin with eight minutes remaining on the clock. To the relief of the All Blacks, and the coaches who could barely see through the steamed-up windows of their box in the stand, the kick missed.

With time almost up on the clock, the All Blacks forwards attacked the Irish line. In the back of many minds was the fact that the dropped goal had never really been part of the All Blacks' match-winning arsenal. But lessons had been learnt from Cardiff five years earlier. The All Black forwards ground their way for position in the centre of the field, rather than risking a concerted attack on the try line. They were setting up for Carter to try to pot a goal.

The pass from Weepu, who had replaced Aaron Smith, was not the best he'd ever delivered, and it put Carter off balance in retrieving it and thus he struggled to set properly for the kick. It flew awkwardly from his right boot and wide of the right upright. Irish fans breathed a sigh of relief, but referee Nigel Owens ruled that the kick had, in fact, been touched in flight by an Irish defender and ruled a five-yard scrum for the All Blacks.

The All Black forwards held steady and the Irish backs knew there was only one man to attack — Carter — who this time would be able to attempt another dropped goal on his preferred left foot. Weepu fired his pass from the base of

the scrum to Carter who kicked. The ball sailed low, wobbling and swerving about in midair before passing through the uprights. The All Blacks had won 22–19, but were made to work very hard to avoid their first loss to Ireland, and what would have been only their second draw against the men in green. Carter later told media, 'We got out of jail.'

As a result of a head-knock, Read was rested from the third test in Hamilton, with McCaw moving to number eight and Sam Cane starting in the number seven jersey. The young open-side had a stellar game in a side full of stars, as the Irish were walloped 60–0! It was their highest losing margin to the All Blacks.

Super Rugby resumed but Read suffered a cracked rib in the Round 15 clash with the Chiefs in Hamilton, won 28–21 by the Crusaders. He subsequently missed the final round robin match, and the play-offs. The Crusaders hosted the Bulls in a quarterfinal (winning 28–13), but lost their semifinal against the Chiefs the following week in Hamilton 17–20. The Waikato franchise would go on to win their first Super Rugby title, overwhelming the Sharks 37–6 in the final.

There was a new challenge for the All Blacks that season with the Tri-Nations morphing into The Rugby Championship, with the addition of Argentina. Since 1976, the All Blacks had only played in Argentina eight times for seven wins and a famous 21–21 draw in 1985. Six of those games were as part of a two-test series, so the visits to play the Pumas in South America were infrequent. Now they would go once a year and

the tournament would be spread over three continents. Great news for airlines!

Read's rib had recovered enough for him to be named in the opening game against Australia in Sydney and he downplayed concerns some had about his lack of game time before facing the Wallabies.

'I don't feel like I need the games to get back up to that level. It's been really good; I've been able to do a lot of reconditioning, a lot of running and weights and they are probably the things I haven't been able to do lately. My fitness is fine and it's just a matter of getting up to test match level.'

The All Blacks triumphed in a tight match 27–19, and then held Australia scoreless in the return match at Eden Park, winning 22–0.

When it came time for Argentina's first act of participating in the tournament, a match against the All Blacks in Wellington, Read was preparing for the game along with his teammates when he received a phone call from Christchurch. Wife Bridget had gone into labour and the arrival of the Reads' second child was imminent!

One marked difference between the amateur and professional sporting eras is the attitude towards players' family lives. In the old days, players would head away on three-month tours to South Africa, or through the United Kingdom, Ireland and France, and miss the birth of their children. Some would lose money through having to take time off from their jobs, or having to pay people to manage their farms while they were away.

It's all very different now. Of course, there is now cheaper and more frequent domestic and international air travel. But the attitude of the All Blacks' employers (New Zealand Rugby) and their immediate bosses (the coaches) means that there is a more holistic view of what is important in the lives of players.

So when Read's wife, Bridget, went into labour, 11 days before the due date, management, who were of course aware of an impending arrival, quickly arranged for him to fly home to Christchurch for the special family event.

Upon landing in Christchurch, Read raced to the hospital in the hope that he would be there in time for the actual birth. He was 10 minutes late but it didn't in any way dampen the joy of seeing his second daughter, Eden.

The next morning, after a somewhat sleepless night, Read had to start thinking about international rugby again and make his way back to Wellington. Here the capital's capricious weather intervened. Due to high winds, he had to fly from Christchurch all the way up to Auckland, then back down to Wellington. He arrived four hours before kick-off. He told Richard Knowler:

> *'It was tough getting the call, trying to shoot down and get back. It was pretty crazy … Once I got back into a routine back at the hotel, I was pretty much thinking about the game. Afterwards you think what a crazy twenty-four hours it was.'*

Adding to the craziness was the fact that at half-time during the game, played in pretty awful weather, the lights had gone out at the stadium as a power cut affected that area of downtown Wellington. Fortunately, power was restored quickly, though the half-time break was extended by 10 minutes as the teams, match officials and spectators waited for the lights to come back up to full beam again.

The following day, after the All Blacks had won 21–5, Read was able to enjoy a couple of days with his wife and children before the All Blacks reassembled in Dunedin for their test against the Springboks. That match was won (21–11) and the team then set off around the southern hemisphere to play Argentina in La Plata (54–15) and the Springboks again in Johannesburg (32–16).

In the Johannesburg match, the All Blacks had been down 12–16 at half-time, but put in a barnstorming second half to score 20 unanswered points. As well as securing the inaugural Rugby Championship with six wins out of six, the win gave McCaw his 100th win in test matches, something no other player had achieved in the history of the game.

Read had a superb game with ball in hand, giving the final pass to Nonu who scored after just 19 seconds in the second half, and then handling twice in a sweeping movement which saw Sam Whitelock lope to the line for a deserved try.

Two weeks later, the team had a third Bledisloe test against Australia at Suncorp Stadium in Brisbane. Despite the fact that the All Blacks had already secured the massive cup for another year, it was a match significant for other milestones. If the All Blacks won, they would equal the world record of 17 consecutive test match wins. They would also beat Australia for the 100th time, in Keven Mealamu's 100th test for the All Blacks.

In the back of the minds of some of the players was the fact that the last time they had played at the ground, prior to the Rugby World

Cup, they had not had a good game against a spirited Wallaby team and lost 25–20. Sam Whitelock told media:

'I played the whole game and it's not nice to lose in the black jersey. Losing to Aussie in Aussie hurts a bit more … we're looking forward to getting over there and trying to right that wrong.'

Great Kieran Read All Blacks Moments #4

Test 43
New Zealand versus South Africa, 21–11
Forsyth Barr Stadium, Dunedin
15 September 2012

Against the Springboks, indoors at Dunedin's Forsyth Barr stadium, the match was tied up at 3–3 after 25 minutes of the match. Following a failed drop-kick attempt by the Springboks, the All Blacks had a drop out from their 22. Aaron Cruden took the kick, hoisting it high towards halfway. Read began his run towards the ball from the left-hand side-line towards the 10-metre line, where his opposite, big Springbok number eight Duane Vermeulen, was calling for the ball. A split second after Vermeulen took the ball, Read barrelled into him, driving his right shoulder into his middle, which knocked Vermeulen backwards onto the ground, leaving him prone to the All Blacks contesting for the ruck ball. But Vermeulen held on to the ball as his teammates flopped over him and referee George Clancy quickly penalised them. Cruden kicked for touch and the All Blacks had gone from one end of the field to the other, thanks to a punishing, perfectly timed and executed tackle from Read.

McCaw tried to play down attention to the possibility of equalling the world record, saying the side had tried to keep it in the back of their minds and focus more on achieving a high standard of play, to match that of their win over South Africa in the Republic.

The canny Wallabies didn't allow the All Black backs any space and the game became one of errors and frustration for the All Blacks. Try as they did, they could not break the shackles of an Australian team that was attacking at the breakdown and quick to pressure them when they tried to move the ball wide.

Keven Mealamu has played more first-class games of rugby than any other New Zealander in a career that began in 1999.

Neither side had scored a try by the time the 80 minutes had elapsed. It was the first time this had happened to the All Blacks in over 100 tests! The scores were level at 18–18, the result of six penalty goals from Carter, five from Wallaby Mike Harris, and one from his teammate Kurtley Beale. Referee Craig Joubert let the game run for four extra minutes and Carter attempted a dropped goal hoping to win the match, but it just flew to the left of the posts. Game over.

Everybody, it seemed, was stunned. The crowd was unusually quiet and players on both sides were supremely disappointed as they knew they had had opportunities to win the game. Several All Blacks later said that the draw felt like a loss, that they were annoyed by the mistakes they had made and sad that they couldn't celebrate Mealamu's milestone with a win. Read even wondered if they had perhaps underestimated the Wallabies. So equalling the world record would have to wait, but at least the side remained unbeaten for the year.

A month after the Brisbane draw (which had seen some commentators calling for a league-like golden point to be introduced to the game), the All Blacks jetted off for their annual end-of-year tour to the northern hemisphere. Before departing, Read told reporters that there was still disappointment in the camp about their performance and that the side preferred to learn from their wins, than from games such as Brisbane. More positively, he said that the upcoming month-long tour would 'hopefully show the people up north how to play the game of rugby, and we want to play a really nice style so hopefully we can do that'.

Read's appointment as captain for one of the tour matches had been flagged before the team left New Zealand and media asked him if being in that position of responsibility would alter his on-field play or style. 'I hope not,' he smiled. 'It's all about doing the business on the field and performing the best you can. Being a leader or not, I try to do that every game.'

He sat out the opening game against Scotland, in which the All Blacks played impressively to win 51–22. The next match was against Italy at the Stadio Olimpico in Rome, and Read, set to play his 46th test, was named (in a side that had 14 changes from the week before) as All Blacks captain for the first time. 'I can't wait to run out at the head of the pack,' he told Sportal.co.nz, 'but it's all about getting my job done so it is pretty important to make sure I do that. It is a great opportunity, a massive honour, and one of the biggest jobs in the country. I'll be following a man, McCaw, who, in my opinion, is the best captain ever in the All Blacks. He told me the easiest way to lead is if you are the best player on the pitch, and I think he does that every week, and that is essentially how I want to do things as well. I have to get my performance right, then the guys will follow and you can lead with your words after that.'

Kieran Read's First Test as Captain

New Zealand versus Italy, 42–10
Rome
18 November 2010

All Blacks
Tony Woodcock, Keven Mealamu, Charlie Faumuina, Ali Williams, Brodie Retallick, Liam Messam, Sam Cane, Kieran Read, Aaron Smith, Aaron Cruden, Julian Savea, Ma'a Nonu, Conrad Smith, Hosea Gear, Beauden Barrett.
Reserves: Dane Coles, Wyatt Crockett, Ben Franks, Sam Whitelock, Victor Vito, Tawera Kerr-Barlow, Dan Carter, Cory Jane.

Opposing him at number eight was Sergio Parisse, who captained his side. Both forwards were well aware of the abilities of the other and looked forward to the individual, as well as the team, match-ups.

The stadium had been the venue for the 1990 FIFA World Cup final and was home to two of the most famous football clubs in Europe: Lazio and Roma. However, it was in front of 75,000 Italian rugby fans that Read led the team onto the field. He scored the opening try of the game, one of five for the All Blacks, but they spent much of the match being harried by the seemingly irrepressible Italians, particularly at the breakdown, where referee Alain Rolland allowed the home side a lot of leeway in his interpretations.

Three All Black tries in the final 15 minutes, including two to Julian Savea, meant a 42–10 score-line, one which it was widely agreed flattered the All Blacks somewhat and didn't reflect the passion the Azzurri had played with. Read told Sky Sport:

> 'It's a great credit to the way they [Italy] have come on in the last few years; it was a really hard game. Sometimes it takes seventy to eighty minutes to get the result.'

Wales was the next opponent, in Cardiff, but an impressive first half in which the All Blacks led 23–0 was overshadowed by hooker Andrew Hore's opening-minute, off-the-ball swinging

The pictures say it all. There was nothing the All Blacks could do to stop a rampant England at Twickenham in 2012.

arm to lock Bradley Davies. Chasing a kick, Hore chose to clock the Welshman rather than push him out of the way and knocked him out, and out of the game. The incident was repeated endlessly in the stadium and in television broadcasts, but somehow Hore stayed on the field. He later served a five-match ban.

As for the match, the All Blacks won 33–10, meaning that with one game left in the 2012 season, against England, they were 80 minutes away from having an unbeaten season. The English went into the game under the blowtorch of their media, having lost to both Australia and South Africa in the preceding weeks.

When the match began, the fervour of the Stewart Lancaster-coached English side was being rewarded with points and they were quickly out to a 12–0 lead. Dan Carter, who had been in doubt for the match due to a muscle twinge at the bottom of one of his legs, was having an off day with his kicking, there seemed to be a constant lack of All Black forwards defending at the breakdown, and the English lead extended to 15–0 not long after half-time. The All Blacks rallied in typical fashion and clawed their way back to 14–15. In the past, this may have unsettled the English, but they regrouped and stormed home in emphatic fashion, including snatching an intercept from a Read pass, to win 38–21.

For the first time since 2002, when England beat them 31–18, the All Blacks lost an end-of-year tour test and suffered their first loss in 20 games. England had also racked up their highest score against them.

The Guardian's Claire Tolley rated Read the best of the All Blacks forwards, writing that he:

> '… had the strongest game of the New Zealand pack, tackling strongly, but one man couldn't stem the tide. Took his try well.'

Fellow *Guardian* writer Paul Rees wrote:

> 'New Zealand were such a shadow of the team that had swept all before them in the previous 16 months that they should have been wearing pale grey. They had been hit in the week by a virus and were anaemic apart from a short try-scoring burst at the start of the second half when they were 15 points down.'

Yes, it was the end of the long test programme and there had been illness in the camp during the week. But credit had to go to England for the barnstorming performance they put on in front of over 82,000 fans, who just could not believe they were watching their side play with such speed, flair and dominance.

McCaw made no excuses, nor did Steve Hansen who, having suffered his first loss as head coach, told media after the match that:

> '… we got beaten by the better side. This is a good England side … They thoroughly deserved their victory and should be proud of what they have achieved with magnificent football. They took the game to us from the get-go, full credit to them … Though it hurts like hell at the moment, it won't do us any harm. It will stop people telling us we're the greatest team ever and all that crap. We'll get down to being an All Black side that has to work hard. We've got to manage the feelings we're having at the moment and put them in the right place so they actually work for us in the future … It's about meeting your own expectations, and tonight we didn't do that. That's the pain we'll take through right into next season. That's the pain that won't do us any harm.'

England captain Chris Robshaw hoists the Hillary Shield after his team's stunning 38–21 victory.

He offered a metaphor of the players spending their summer thinking about that Twickenham loss being like a rock under their beach towels.

In a review of the 2012 season, *NZ Rugby World* magazine named Read as one of their five Players of the Year.

> *'There are many similarities between Kieran Read and McCaw — the most notable being their desire to be consistently excellent. Read is not happy to play well one week and disappear the next. He's a front-every-test sort of guy and he managed that this year. He didn't have a bad game and had a number of outstanding ones. He thunders about the place and his tackling may have gained in intensity this year. His leadership, drive and experience made him look more like the captain-in-waiting. He's so calm, measured and certain that it would be impossible not to want to play for him. The part of his game that advanced most was his ability to play with the ball on the edges of the defence. He spent more time getting wider where he was harder to stop. He looms as the obvious stand-in captain for McCaw when the latter has a sabbatical next year.'*

The editors of the *Rugby Almanack of New Zealand* similarly acknowledged his performances throughout the year.

McCaw ponders the Twickenham loss and his side missing out on an unbeaten 2012 season. The challenge of a perfect season remained.

'With many young players, potential is something that has not been achieved. In Kieran's case, that potential has been delivered into products of excellence in every step of his career to the extent that he is now regarded as one of the best, if not the best number eight playing in world rugby today … There is more to come. His achievements have been hard-earned and will not be relinquished lightly.'

The year after a side wins the Rugby World Cup can bring them back to earth pretty quickly, but the All Blacks' year was a success. They had a new coach, and had played 14 tests in eight countries for 12 wins, a loss and a draw.

Read reflected on the Twickenham loss, telling TVNZ:

'You always look back at your last result. She could be a pretty awkward summer. There will be a few thoughts going around in the mind for a bit. It gives you a bit to ponder. I haven't finished this way for my whole career so we'll see how it pans out.'

When it came to Read's rise as a player, the old cliché was about to be applied: you ain't seen nothing yet!

A Team Unbeaten and the Best Player in the World

The Crusaders' 2013 Super Rugby season came to a disappointing end in the semifinals when they lost to the Chiefs (19–20), having beaten the eventual champions 43–15 three weeks earlier.

Kieran Read's First Home Test as Captain

New Zealand versus France, 23–13
Eden Park, Auckland
8 June 2013

All Blacks
Wyatt Crockett, Dane Coles, Owen Franks, Luke Romano, Brodie Retallick, Liam Messam, Sam Cane, Kieran Read, Aaron Smith, Aaron Cruden, Julian Savea, Ma'a Nonu, Conrad Smith, Ben Smith, Israel Dagg. Reserves: Keven Mealamu, Ben Franks, Ben Afeaki, Jeremy Thrush, Victor Vito, Tawera Kerr-Barlow, Beauden Barrett, Rene Ranger.

In years to come, a good rugby trivia question might be: 'Who captained the All Blacks in their 500th test?' Answer: Kieran Read, deputising for McCaw who was enjoying a rugby-free sabbatical. This was in the second All Black test of the year when they faced the French in Christchurch (having beaten them the week before in Auckland by 23–13, when Read captained the All Blacks in a home test for the first time, watched by his family in the stands).

There was another milestone with the All Blacks keeping the French scoreless for the first time in their 53 encounters, stretching way back to 1906. 'I'm extremely happy,' said Read post-match. 'The effort we put in in defence really showed the character we have got. It's not easy on a night like this and the boys really stepped up.'

When Read led the All Blacks out onto Yarrow Stadium a week later for the final test of the 2013 French visit, he was running on turf that his uncle Bill (brother of Read's father, Terry) knew every centimetre of. He had been the groundsman at the New Plymouth ground (formerly known as Rugby Park) for three decades, and the fact that his nephew would be leading the All Blacks in a rare test match at the venue was a source of great pride. Interviewed for the New Zealand Sports Turf Institute website, Bill said:

> 'When I've been driving around doing the mowing it's been in the back of my mind all the time. It adds a bit of pride to my job. It's an awesome feeling. I'm really looking forward to it. Like all the family, we've followed Kieran with great interest. He's reached the pinnacle. Captaining the All Blacks ... it doesn't get much better.'

Great Kieran Read All Blacks Moments #5

Test 51
New Zealand versus France, 30–0
AMI Stadium, Christchurch
15 June 2013

Captaining the All Blacks against France in Christchurch, the All Blacks led 7–0 after 20 minutes of the first half. The French were on attack but failed to follow up a penalty kick, which bounced off the left-hand upright back into the field of play. Conrad Smith caught the ball five metres from his own try line. Seeing that the approaching French players were still about 10 metres away, he passed infield to his right, where Read took the ball at pace and set off on a scything run upfield. He beat as many as six would-be tacklers, and fended off two before being tackled just over the halfway line.

The match itself was won 24–9 by the All Blacks, but large parts of the game were ordinary compared to their efforts of the previous week. Hansen, however, was very happy with the series result and the fact that Read had:

> '... been outstanding in this campaign. He's led well. He's responded to the challenge of leadership by playing well. We've known he's a world-class player for some time now and this series has reinforced that. He's a pretty vital ingredient to our team. There's many spokes that make the world go round but his spoke is an important one. He has a presence on the park in every test. He's set a standard and we've just got to keep maintaining that.'

McCaw came back into the side to captain two wins over Australia: 47–29 in Sydney, and 27–16 in Wellington. (The Wallabies were now coached by Ewen McKenzie, following the resignation of Robbie Deans after the 1–2 series loss to the British and Irish Lions.) In the next match, against Argentina in Hamilton, McCaw injured a medial ligament in his knee, which put him on the side-lines for several weeks.

Steve Hansen unreservedly backed Read to take over the captaincy again in McCaw's absence, telling reporter Liam Napier:

> 'Reado is well established. We're getting performances from him as we expect. We think he's probably the best number eight in the world at the moment. He didn't let us down. He probably went up a gear when the skipper went off. That's what you want to see. You want your best players to find something extra when you lose another top guy.'

Read captained the side against the Springboks with the visitors leading the Rugby Championship by a point from the All Blacks. Further motivation for the South Africans and their emotional coach, Heyneke Meyer, was that a win would see them become the top-ranked side in world rugby, a position the All Blacks had been in for four years.

Read told media that the All Blacks:

'… love playing here at Eden Park. It certainly is our home here in New Zealand, but I think it's more about us coming out and performing and doing what we can. I guess if we keep winning, that's what we want to do. It's awesome to be at Eden Park, from our point of view. I guess it's our biggest test for a long time so we're really looking forward to it. They still pride themselves on their set piece and chasing kicks and being physical, and that's something they will continue to do. I guess they have shown they can play with the ball and score tries, which is a threat as well, but I would expect them to still come at us in the forwards so that's the challenge for the boys up front. It's certainly a big challenge. I think both teams are playing pretty good rugby at the moment. Both camps have got a bit of confidence. As a team, we know the challenges ahead but we're confident in our abilities and know that we can play a lot better than we have done. So it's going to be a good test.'

It was for Read, and for the All Blacks. They won 29–15 with Read scoring two tries.

After the match, in which Bismarck du Plessis controversially received two yellow cards and thus had to leave the field, Read said:

'Certainly, the intensity of the test match was the highest we have had this year, and I think our performance was the best we have produced. The 'Boks play physically and our tight five really stepped up and got us on the front foot … no one was going to give an inch … [and] we certainly didn't take a step back.'

One of the areas where the All Blacks had markedly improved over the previous few years was the lineout. The word 'wobbles' had so often been associated with it, and there were times when the lack of confidence in tight situations by those throwing the ball to the lineout, and those lined up as part of it, seemed obvious to all. Something had to be done as it couldn't remain a phase where securing possession was a lottery. Hansen had studied the Springbok lineout, which was a successful mix of two simple things: the timing of the throw, and two big men lifting another big man.

When lifting in the lineout finally became a legal part of the game, the theory was to use men who can't jump, i.e. props, to lift those that can. So the front-rowers, not renowned for their height, were lifting the locks. The next innovation became using locks and flankers to lift other locks and flankers. Read has been one of the key participants in the change of fortunes of the All Black lineout, as both the caller at the set piece, and a catcher. Often he lines up between two locks, let's say, Brodie Retallick and Sam Whitelock, giving the All Blacks a range of options. Read can be a lifter of either of those men, or be lifted himself. The latter has been the option many a time in crucial situations.

Hansen, in conversation with *Herald* rugby writer Gregor Paul, reviewed the development of the lineout:

'Our lineout, from a height point of view, is very, very good. I think they [the four locks] are complemented too by Reado [Kieran Read] and Steve Luatua when he gets out there — big, big loose forwards as well. In 2009, we changed our structure. We changed our basic skills. We had a lot of guys double-jumping. We were really slow in the air. Our lifting technique was poor and, when you are changing things, it takes time. In World Cup year, we were averaging high eighty per cent from our lineout returns, which was one of the best in the world. Last year [2012], we were the leading lineout in the southern hemisphere — we were averaging in the nineties. Not only winning ball at ninety per cent, but top-quality ball on top of that. In the first test [against France, 2013], we were down in the seventies, and that is not good enough. That's not where we expect to be but, when we went through the clips, there were some obvious flaws in what we are doing and we have crept back into some old habits. I think it is just human nature: if you look at golfers and their swing ... little things creep in. It is no one's fault, it is just what happens, and I think that is what has happened with some of our lineout skills. So we have had an emphasis on getting back to our explosive jumping; getting our lifters on and speeding the whole thing up and I am positive we will get a big improvement. If you can get your

*set piece right, and if you include your
restarts in that and let's chuck
the breakdown in there as well, then
you have got four areas where you
can dominate games. You have to
have a platform to build anything on.
It goes back to your tight five and loose
forwards doing their jobs well, and it
is the old, old cliché of winning games
up front.'*

The All Black lineout had improved so much
that even Victor Matfield, arguably the greatest
lineout presence in the professional era,
acknowledged its strength and pointed to Read
as being crucial to it.

On 5 October 2013, the All Blacks and South
Africa played one of the truly great tests of the
modern era, a game every bit as gripping as the
phenomenal 39–35 clash between the All Blacks
and Australia in front of 110,000 in Sydney 13
years earlier. The All Blacks won that game in the
final minute with Jonah Lomu daintily avoiding
the touchline to score. It was a game the young
Kieran had been captivated by.

Much credit for the openness of the match
in South Africa has to go to the Springboks and
coach Meyer, who was a proponent of a more
expansive game plan than the traditional 'Bok
reliance on a constantly kicking first-five. They
went into the game knowing that they could
swipe the Rugby Championship title from the All
Blacks if they won with a bonus point.

There was a time when All Black wins at
Ellis Park, Johannesburg, were hard to come
by. It remains a ground where the South
Africans seem to play with a greater physical
intensity, spurred on by frenzied crowds. A win
for the home side is never out of the question,
particularly, as on this occasion, the All Blacks
had played in Argentina the week before for a

33–15 win. The match at the Estadio Ciudad in
La Plata saw the All Blacks needing a win and a
bonus point to put extra pressure on the South
Africans in the final game. A Ben Smith try
minutes from the end of the game secured five
championship points.

So one week South America, the next South
Africa …

The flight time between the two continents
is only nine hours — not quite long enough for
the players to get a decent sleep — and time
differences mean they arrive early in the morning
and are then up all day. So it takes a couple of
days for the players to physically settle back into
the routine of test preparation. Graham Henry
had previously spoken to Gregor Paul about the
difficulties of taking an international rugby side to
South Africa:

*'It is not an easy country to be in. We
are conscious of security, that there is
a lot of crime, and you don't always feel
comfortable in Johannesburg, so everyone
has to make good decisions. It makes it
hard to get away from the hotel and it can
make for a long week. You also have a few
physical challenges, as you can't really
overdo it in training in a physical sense as it
is only about the Thursday that the players
are coming right.'*

Read, who exhibits an excitement about
upcoming matches in a way few of his peers do,
told Paul:

*'I do enjoy playing there. We play in
the afternoon so the ball is dry and
the ground is hard … I think the crowd
can be a motivating factor for us. I love
having that noise and that intensity, as it
lifts my game.'*

The fleet-footed Beauden Barrett made a habit of try-scoring cameos.

The real challenge for the 'Boks was whether they could keep the ball in hand and score the requisite four tries against an All Black team that had conceded an average of fewer than 18 points through that year's Rugby Championship, while scoring an average of almost 33 points per game.

From the opening whistle, the men of the Republic showed that they weren't going to die wondering. Their forwards charged into their work, hoping to physically intimidate their All Black opposites and create momentum in getting over the advantage line, which would then allow their backs to run into space created by back-pedalling defenders. The only problem with that plan was that the All Blacks, and particularly the tight five, weren't going to be at all compliant with their hosts' plans, regardless of the physical toll it took on them. Players wearing the low numbers collided, on and off the ball, with an intensity that would have made a couple of angry rhinos wince! The loose forwards pounced on

the ball, and each other, while the backs eagerly looked for space behind and between defensive lines.

Referee Nigel Owens, renowned for his overly judicious whistling, which can cause games to be more stop-start than a car being pushed uphill, played his part too. He was a revelation, allowing the game to flow to such an extent that spectators were left breathless, let alone the aerobic toll it was taking on the 30 players on the field.

It was a magnificent, exhilarating game with both teams retaining the ball for numerous phases and play swinging wildly from one end of the field to the other. Fans didn't dare leave their seats, and television viewers didn't dare blink for fear of missing a key moment.

South Africa had scored their four tries with half an hour of the game still to play. But the All Blacks were getting over the line, too. Ben Smith had finished a sweeping move, taking the final pass from Read who, in what had become a new positional tactic, had charged down the tramlines holding the ball in two hands, drawing in defenders. Messam bagged a double, while Beauden Barrett came on and, within minutes, made one of his typical gap-finding runs that may have had some of his teammates wondering why they were having such difficulty breaking the defensive line. His try gave the All Blacks a bonus point and the match was sealed for McCaw's men (with a final score of 38–27) when Read scored the final try of the match.

It was a fitting end to the game, given that Read was universally praised for his all-round performance. In a match where men from both teams were playing out of their skins, he truly shone. Crunching tackles, lineout takes, charges from the back of the scrum, deft passes, breakdown steals, long striding runs … he was an omnipresent threat.

Test 58
New Zealand versus South Africa, 38–27
Ellis Park, Johannesburg
5 October 2013

With just 10 minutes gone in the scintillating encounter with the Springboks at Ellis Park, Read took a pass at pace 15 metres in from touch on the South African 10-metre line. He fended off flanker William Alberts and charged on. Just short of the 22-metre line, Bryan Habana came in off his wing to try to stop Read. In contact, Read flicked a short pass out of the back of his right hand to Ben Smith, who cut inside two would-be tacklers and scored a great try. Seventy minutes later, Read was being hailed as having played a '10 out of 10' game, in a match that is now regarded as one of the greats of the professional era.

While he would be quick to deflect praise from his individual efforts, his was one of the great performances on the world rugby stage. The *New Zealand Herald* player ratings for the match saw Read given a rare 10 out of 10 by columnist Chris Rattue. In a piece dedicated to Read, Rattue wrote:

> 'His still-growing leadership influence matches Lochore, he has the power and authority of Buck, plus the skills of Zinny. The Cantabrian wonder has got it all and these various attributes came together in the toughest of cauldrons, Ellis Park, in a magnificent test match against South Africa. Read stood head and shoulders above the rest … Read, the captain-in-waiting, never missed a beat. The man is an absolute marvel, and with a World Cup medal in the drawer, this game elevates him to a place where he can be anointed as the All Black No 8 supreme. His raw-boned athleticism is vastly superior to his predecessors, as is his impact across so many areas.'

Players love to be part of matches like that to showcase just how exciting the game of rugby can be at the highest level. After the match, McCaw told media:

> 'I think it was a great spectacle for fans. They are big boys, those South African lads, and you have to meet fire with fire. I think the tight five really stood up today and set up a platform so us loosies could do what we do.'

A win (41–33) over Australia in Dunedin followed before the end-of-year tour began playing Japan in Tokyo. Read was rested for the game at the Prince Chibu Memorial Stadium, won by the All Blacks by 54–6. He returned to the side for the 26–19 win over France in Paris. The All Blacks then crossed the English Channel to meet England at Twickenham.

Prior to that, Read told reporters:

> 'I feel like I have grown my game, and that the way we're playing is showcasing what I do. I want to have that influence. Every time I go on the field, I'm looking to be the man who is the key factor in the game, who can make a big play or whatever is needed. I want to do my bit.'

Great Kieran Read All Blacks Moments #7

Test 61
New Zealand versus England, 30–22
Twickenham, England
16 November 2013

Less than two minutes into the game against England at Twickenham, and after a scrappy lineout five metres from the English try line and disruptive defence from the English forwards, Aaron Smith opted to pass to a narrow blindside where McCaw, Carter, Read and Savea stood. McCaw swung a quick pass to Carter, who just got the ball away in a tackle, but it bounced before getting to Read. He scooped it up and ran a short diagonal line towards the left-hand corner flag. Two other English players joined the tackling wing, attempting to push Read out. But, just as he was about to cross the touchline, he hooked a right-hand pass behind and infield to Savea, who crossed the English try line without a hand being laid on him. Was the pass a fluke, a piece of luck? Not at all. Read had thrown another 'miracle pass' against Argentina in Hamilton two months earlier in setting up a try for Aaron Smith.

Nonu cuts through the French defence.

The All Blacks had early points on the board thanks to Savea. They were added to in the 16th minute after Owen Franks made a break any midfield back would be proud of. The quickly recycled ball went to the right-running Dagg on the English 22. He drew a defender and slipped a pass to Read, who easily broke one tackle and stormed to the line. It was his 15th try in tests, breaking Zinzan Brooke's record of 14 for most test tries by an All Black number eight. (He is still well off the overall record held by Uruguayan Diego Ormaechea, who in 49 matches between 1983 and 1999 scored 29 test tries.)

England were on the back foot, down 19–7 at one stage, but closed the game up to 20–22. A second try to Savea saw the All Blacks win 30–22.

The final test for the All Blacks in 2013 was against Ireland at Aviva Stadium in Dublin. Nearly 52,000 vocal fans were positively roaring as Ireland began with the sort of scoring onslaught the All Blacks are only rarely on the receiving end of. Within 20 minutes the Irish were leading 19–0 and the belief seemed to be growing within the players and the fans that for the first time in 28 tests, dating back to their first encounter in 1905, an Irish win could become a reality.

But the All Blacks hadn't won their previous 12 tests (with an average score of 31 points) by mere fluke. They were a team around which Hansen had built a plan to achieve the perfect season. They certainly didn't want to repeat the massive fall at the final hurdle they'd had against England at the end of the previous season.

While the Irish put personal safety last as they tore into the breakdown and made fearless tackles, McCaw's men absorbed the pressure and then began to turn it back onto the Irish, who knew full well that an All Black riposte would come. Over the years, many have joked that if rugby was a 60-minute game, the Irish would be world champions. Inspirational Irish skipper, lock Paul O'Connell, led the charge, exhorting his men on. Loose forwards Sean O'Brien and Jamie Heaslip kept barrelling into the breakdown and first-five Johnny Sexton had the ball on a string, with kicks for territory in behind the All Blacks. Veteran centre, the great Brian O'Driscoll — playing his last test against the All Blacks — marshalled those around him and, in trademark fashion, shadowed his opposites and worked his way over the advantage line with ball in hand.

The All Blacks began their claw-back, thanks to a try to Savea but, by half-time, they were still down 7–22. Cruden kicked a penalty and, with 15 minutes to play, Ben Franks scored a try and the score closed to 17–22. The All Blacks needed a converted try for the win. The Irish needed a penalty or a dropped goal to push them that little further out of reach and closer to victory.

With four minutes to go, referee Nigel Owens saw the All Blacks infringe at a maul. Here was the match-winning chance. Sexton placed the ball just outside the All Blacks' 22 and 10 metres in from touch. As the ball rose from the kicking tee, the crowd behind the posts began to cheer. It looked as though it was going over. Then it just faded away to the right.

'It was pretty tight, wasn't it?' said Read after the game. 'I was off to halfway because I thought [Sexton] got it, to be honest. I was about thirty to forty metres gone and then I had to trek back to the twenty-two. I guess we still believed and wanted to back ourselves. That was probably a game-changer that miss, if you look back on it. It kept us in the game and we showed how much ticker and how much fight we've got in us.'

So there was still time for the All Blacks but they had to get the ball, and Ireland, once they had it in their possession, were going to bury it deep in the forwards' huddle and make sure the All Blacks couldn't get their hands on it. As the Irish swayed forward looking to run down the clock, referee Owens awarded a penalty to the All Blacks on their own 10-metre line. There was no time available for them to kick to a lineout. They had to keep ball in hand and travel 60 metres for a try *and* conversion to win the game.

Great Kieran Read All Blacks Moments #8

Test 62
New Zealand versus Ireland, 24–22
Aviva Stadium, Dublin
24 November 2013

With 30 seconds left to play against Ireland, the All Blacks were seconds away from again missing out on going through the year unbeaten, and being the first side in the professional era to do so. Referee Nigel Owens awarded the All Blacks a penalty on their 10-metre line and they had no option but to run the ball. Smith took a quick tap and the All Blacks began their movement up-field. Nearly two minutes later, hooker Dane Coles found himself metres from the line in a two-on-one situation with Crotty outside him. He slipped a short pass to Crotty who scored just in from the left-hand corner. Read had handled twice in that astounding final passage of play, making ground each time, as well as throwing an offload.

Aaron Cruden had two chances to turn a draw into a win against Ireland in Dublin in 2013.

That's exactly what they did, retaining the ball for *two minutes*. Then Nonu controlled a bouncing pass inside the Irish 22. From the ruck, Aaron Smith cleared to Cruden, who had Read, Dane Coles and Crotty outside him. As two Irish defenders eyed Read, Cruden threw a skip pass to Coles who had Crotty outside him with one man to beat. Hooker Coles slipped a short pass to Crotty, who scored just in from the corner. Irish hearts were broken. The scores were tied.

But there was still more drama to come. Cruden had a left-hand side-line conversion to win the game.

His kicking style has caught a few teams out during his time in international rugby. He steps back from the ball and then, after he has set himself, readjusts his feet. To those defenders on the goal-line, it looks as though he is about to approach the ball and kick. So many times opposing players have run out early, attempting to charge his kick, which goes against one of the oldest rules in the rugby book.

That is exactly what happened on this occasion. Several Irish players ran towards Cruden before he had begun moving into his kicking stride, which was noted by referee Owens. The kick sailed across the posts and away to the right. The Irish crowd thought the game was over and a draw was secured.

Owens whistled, not for the end of the game, but for Cruden to take another kick, and this time the Irish did not have the privilege of charging the kick. Nervously, Cruden struck the ball, which flew right between the middle of the posts. The All Blacks had won, 24–22! They had made it through the year *unbeaten*. The crowd couldn't believe it. Some booed Owens.

The players couldn't believe it either. The All Blacks and their reserves rejoiced. O'Connell's men doubled over, hands on knees, or slunk to the ground in utter dismay.

Steve Hansen made his way to the field to be with his victorious team but, first of all, applauded the Irish team as they walked off, commiserating with several of the players. He told Sky Sport that the biggest thing for him had been the 'mental fortitude they had shown to win the game'. He also said that despite their win in that match, and their record over the year, it was incumbent on his men to remain humble.

McCaw gave deserved credit to the Irish team for putting his players under pressure but praised his side for their composure. He even recalled one of his first games for Canterbury when the red and blacks, led by Todd Blackadder, were down by more than 20 points. Blackadder told his team they could win the game. They did. McCaw never forgot it. 'We got one chance and we took it.'

'You can say a lot,' said Read after the match, 'but you have to look at yourself and if you are exuding a little bit of confidence and the leaders are calm and collected and giving the right messages, the guys feed off it and that's what we tried to do in the second half. We back ourselves — our shape, our game plan, our skills. We had it in us, I guess — but 19 points is a hell of a lead to give. You look at what we have created this year and we didn't want to give up. We have the talent and the skill and pretty much everything we needed to win.'

In a column for the *Sunday Times* newspaper, former England and Lions loose forward Lawrence Dallaglio — a brutally powerful number eight in his day — said:

> 'Before this match no one would have disagreed with the contention that [Read] is the best number eight in the world. I would go further than that. He is the best rugby player in the world.'

It was tremendous praise from a man who was never one to take a step back during his 12-year test career, which saw him capped 85 times for his country, and three times for the British and Irish Lions.

Dallaglio's former England and Lions teammate Will Greenwood picked up on his old mate's comments in a column for the *Telegraph* newspaper, devoted to the importance of Read to the All Blacks in 2013:

> 'At the heart of what they do is Read. Be as cynical as you want about their dressing room hyperbole, about being the most dominant team in history. Ignore the fact that often the most painful phrases are the ones that contain the most truth. But don't pretend that in Read the All Blacks have anything less than a once in a generation player in his position … very few [players] can deliver the magic with such consistency. And that really is what makes him such a class act; his ability to deliver day in day out, game in game out.

Greenwood concluded by describing Read as 'the metronome that makes the All Blacks tick'.

Former All Black loose forward Taine Randell, who captained the side 27 times during his 61-game career between 1997 and 2002, wrote of Read in his *Sunday-Star Times* newspaper column as:

> 'a colossus in a great All Blacks year … He has brought a timeless style to the number eight jersey, a position that has been a tricky area for the All Blacks over recent years … Some number eights

are ball players who love to hit it up,
others like to range wide. Read does
both and he's magnificent on defence
and a lineout option as well. He brings
the absolute full scope to this position.'

The annual award for the best rugby player in
the world has had several name variations since
its inception in 2001, such as IRB International
Player of the Year, and IRB World Rugby Player
of the Year. It is the highest accolade for
international rugby players, given out by the
game's governing body at the same time as
other awards recognising excellence among
players, referees and volunteers.

Read was a 2013 nominee, along with
Eben Etzebeth (South African lock), Sergio
Parisse (inspirational Italian captain and number
eight), Leigh Halfpenny (mercurial Welsh and
Lions fullback), and Ben Smith (outstanding
Highlanders and All Blacks fullback/wing and
prolific try-scorer).

Steve Hansen told Gregor Paul of the *New
Zealand Herald*:

*'Reado should be named the player
of the year, if they're doing their work
right. He's had an outstanding year and
he's probably the best player in the
world at the moment.'*

While Read was undoubtedly honoured to be nominated in the category of Player of the Year, it was still a surprise to him to be named the winner. His notification didn't come at an awards ceremony where his peers donned their best dinner suits and their partners their best dresses for a night out, rather it apparently came simply by text. He told Radio Live Sport:

> 'It's a proud moment to get the recognition. It was a great year for the All Blacks and it makes me feel really proud. Awards are just part and parcel of what you do on the pitch. Getting the opportunity to captain the All Blacks was awesome. I think it gives you confidence when you are out there on the field to lead and really play as best you can.'

He also added, 'It's fun playing for the All Blacks.'

It was a very good year for New Zealand rugby, as awards were also given to the All Blacks (International Team of the Year for the fourth year in a row), Steve Hansen (Coach of the Year for the second time), Tim Mikkelson (International Sevens Player of the Year), and Kayla McAlister (Women's Sevens Player of the Year), and Beauden Barrett's touchdown against France in the 30–0 whitewash was awarded Try of the Year.

Read was also named International Players' Choice Player of the Year and, soon after, the Canterbury Supreme Sportsman of the Year.

Two days after being named the best player in the world, he was awarded the Kel Tremain trophy as the New Zealand Player of the Year, for the second time. At the awards ceremony he told Sky Sports' Scotty Stevenson:

> 'Growing up watching Zinny, hearing about Buck and how much those guys did for the All Blacks and this nation … just to be recognised alongside them is awesome. I can't say I'd ever think that I'd be in this position and I'm certainly loving every minute of it … To lead the nation is inspiring; it's humbling. It just makes you want to do the best you can. You don't want to let anyone down. I know my family are very proud and certainly get a big kick out of it as well. It's a special time to be playing in this jersey at the moment. Coach has done such a great job of creating an environment … it's bloody enjoyable to go out there and play. Not only play, but train and be a part of it, which I guess is why we do this. I can't really call it a job because it is so much fun. I love it.'

He also told Sportinglife.com that:

> 'People will talk about how good this team is, but our job is to go out and win test matches. We've created a real bond in this squad and we're right up there with everyone able to do the job. You can't look too far ahead in this game; you've got to adapt and change. Play like we did this year next year, and it won't be good enough. Teams are improving all the time, so we've got to keep doing that too. That's one thing we've learned over the years.'

IRB Rugby Players of the Year 2001–2014

2001
Keith Wood (Ireland)
Rampaging hooker known as much for his bald pate as for his desire to run with the ball. He captained Ireland, representing his country 58 times between 1994 and 2003, and also played for the British and Irish Lions in 1997 and 2001. He holds the record for the most test tries by a hooker, with 15.

2002
Fabien Galthié (France)
One of France's greatest halfbacks, he played 64 tests between 1991 and 2003, none better perhaps than the 1999 win over the All Blacks in the semifinal of the World Cup. The same year he won, France was the champion northern hemisphere side, winning all of their Six Nations games.

2003
Jonny Wilkinson (England)
Famous for his last-gasp drop goal to win the 2003 Rugby World Cup, Wilkinson eventually played 91 games for England between 1998 and 2011, and he also represented the British and Irish Lions. He was the record point-scorer in tests with 1172, until surpassed by Dan Carter.

2004
Schalk Burger (South Africa)
The fearless loose forward, whose destructive tackling and determination at the breakdown saw him named as South Africa's Rugby Player of the Year, won the award only a year after he had debuted for the Springboks!

2005
Dan Carter (New Zealand)

Many say that Dan Carter never played better than in 2005 when phenomenal performances against the British and Irish Lions, including an incredible 33-point haul in the second test in Wellington, saw him acclaimed as one of the greatest players New Zealand had produced.

2006
Richie McCaw (New Zealand)
McCaw became the regular captain of the All Blacks in 2006 and led the All Blacks to a win in the Tri-Nations, and an undefeated northern hemisphere tour. After being on the shortlist three times, the award was finally his.

2007
Bryan Habana (South Africa)
A key figure in the Springboks 2007 World Cup win, the speedy winger with impeccable timing for intercepts had also had a great Super 14 season with the championship-winning Bulls.

2008
Shane Williams (Wales)
The most-capped Welsh winger was first selected to play for the Red Dragons in 1999 by then Welsh coach Graham Henry. He holds Welsh records for tries in the Six Nations and Rugby World Cup. A nippy player unafraid to mix it with the big men on the field, Williams played on three British and Irish Lions tours.

2009
Richie McCaw (New Zealand)
The All Black captain's second win.

2010
Richie McCaw (New Zealand)
The All Black captain's remarkable third win.

2011
Thierry Dusautoir (France)
The dogged French captain, who had played for France since 2006, scored a try and was named Man of the Match in the Rugby World Cup final at Eden Park. He also dotted down against the All Blacks in the 2007 World Cup quarterfinal in Cardiff.

2012
Dan Carter (New Zealand)
The second win for the greatest points-scorer in the history of rugby.

2013
Kieran Read (New Zealand)

2014
Brodie Retallick (New Zealand)
The towering 23-year-old lock, born in Rangiora and a key component of the Chiefs Super Rugby side, enthralled rugby fans around the world with his dominance at the lineout, his physical presence at rucks and maul, and stampeding runs in broken play. Having played 39 tests since his debut in 2012, graduating from the New Zealand Under 20 side, Retallick has had issues with concussion but has a huge future in international rugby ahead of him.

Concussion

Read began the 2014 Super 15 season carrying the new label of 'World Rugby Player of the Year' and facing a demanding Crusaders Super Rugby campaign, followed by an international season where, a year out from the next Rugby World Cup, the All Blacks would aim to have a second unbeaten season.

Read reflected on past Super Rugby successes and, as Crusaders captain, looked at the upcoming season in an interview with the *Herald*'s Campbell Burnes:

> 'It's a tough competition, and probably winning it in my second year when I was still quite young, you don't realise how much work goes into winning these titles. So you've got to be consistent over the whole year. That's what has let us down in the past — we've made finals, but scraped in and been away in the crucial semifinal or final. That's why the Chiefs have done so well in the last two years, their consistency through the season, to host the final. We've got to keep working on it, and I would love to win another title.'

While some players can look as though they are easing themselves into long seasons and seem to be still in beach cricket mode when Super Rugby begins in the notoriously warm summer month of February, such an approach isn't part of Read's makeup. He told Burnes:

> 'If you're out there playing, you have to be giving it a hundred per cent. If you play well early, then you will reap the benefit later in the year, and it benefits the franchise. I love playing for the Crusaders so it's not too hard to get up for those games, and leading the team as well makes you really on song and doing what you need to be doing.'

The season began on a celebratory note for Read in March when he led the Crusaders onto the field against the Hurricanes at AMI Stadium. He became the 33rd player to clock up 100 Super Rugby games.

After the match (which, unfortunately, the Crusaders lost 26–29), he was presented with a greenstone mere by Rugby Union chairman Mike Eagle. Rugby Union chief executive Steve Tew spoke to the crowd and described Read as:

'... one of those unique players who we have been fortunate enough to watch as he gets better and better. He is a dynamic player who lifts the game every time he steps onto the field.'

Crusaders Coach, Todd Blackadder, added that:

'Reado is a truly world-class player in every respect. Nobody works harder than Kieran off the field or is more committed on the field. He gives everything to this team and is held in incredibly high regard as a result. He is a leader that the players want to listen to and want to make proud.'

Overshadowed by the celebrations was the fact that Read had failed a concussion test during the match. A slow recovery meant he was unavailable to play the following week. Read's season started to go awry.

When he did return to the field he received a swinging arm to his jaw from Chiefs lock Mike Fitzgerald during a very physical game in Hamilton, the effects of which were greater than those watching at the time thought when he failed a side-line concussion test. (Read was one of three to suffer concussion in that match, with Chiefs players Liam Messam and Tawera Kerr-Barlow also being removed from the game after head clashes.)

One of the recent major issues facing both rugby codes is that of head injuries to players, both the effects during games, and later in life. A number of high-profile players who had suffered a series of concussions had what was known as 'footballers' migraines' (which for some saw the end of their playing days), and they continued in their lives post-retirement from the sport. The International Rugby Players Association had been

agitating for several years to see improvements to protocols around players returning to the field if they had suffered a suspected concussion, and stand-down periods for those who had. As such, the Pitch-side Suspected Concussion Assessment was implemented in 2012 to help on-field medical staff diagnose concussed players. The effects of concussion can be visible to spectators (such as a player staggering about the field or not being able to stand up after a head clash), or invisible (with the concussed individual feeling nausea, forgetting where they are, or having ringing in their ears).

One of the ways for team doctors to assess whether a player has suffered a serious head knock is to ask a player five questions about the game they are playing:

What ground are we at?
Which team are we playing today?
Who are you marking?
Which half is it?
What is the score?

If injured players fail to answer even one of these questions correctly, medical staff remove them from the field.

New Zealand Rugby, in line with IRB regulations, brought in mandatory stand-down periods for players of 21 days, which included 14 days of rest, then four days of non-contact training, and, before returning to the field, players had to be free of symptoms for 24 hours.

The symptoms for concussed players are greatly worrying to them and medical staff the longer they go on: not being able to concentrate on what they are doing, constant headaches, dizzy spells and even not being able to sit up quickly after lying down.

Like most players, Read had suffered knocks to the head before but, given his recovery had been speedy, he considered them to be quite minor. But in this case, over the course of

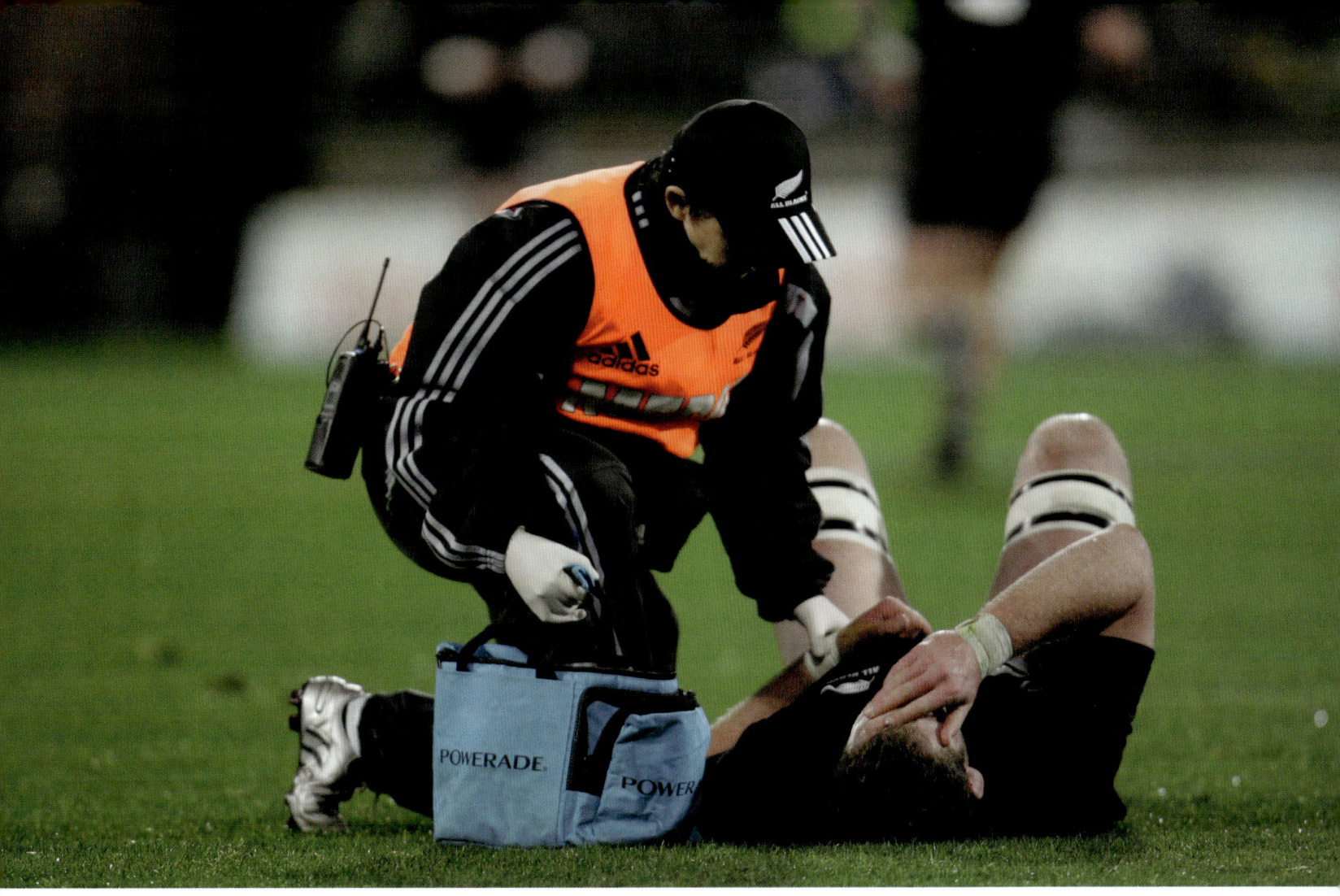

the following month Read was still struggling with the after-effects, and was being closely monitored by the Crusaders doctor, Deb Robinson, who would communicate Read's state of health to Blackadder and the coaching staff.

As Read's return to the field was postponed week after week, there were even calls from some in the sports media for Read to retire and not risk any further head injuries.

'Certainly, it's a worrying injury any time you get one,' Read told Christchurch rugby writer Tony Smith. 'But if you do the process right, and you're honest in how you're feeling … I know Deb's going to look after me and make sure I get back on the field a hundred per cent ready

to go. There is worry, definitely, from my wife, but I know Deb's doing a great job with me and I don't want to put myself at risk. It's one of those injuries where you don't want to risk it anyway. The doc and the coaches are doing the best thing for me.'

Robinson considered the lingering effects to be at 'a very low level', but because it was the second concussion he had suffered in quick succession she deemed that she and Read needed to be a bit more cautious, rather than ambitious, about when he could next take to the field. 'We're very aware he's got a lot of rugby to play this year so we want to look after him well,' said Robinson.

With Todd Blackadder waiting on assessments of Read to see when he could name his captain in his team again, he told media that Read 'hasn't been able to fully participate in contact training for a little while so we're better off giving him more space and time to get back to a hundred per cent'.

Also being regularly updated was All Blacks coach Steve Hansen, who was shortly to name his team for the first test against the visiting England team.

After six weeks on the side-line Read could finally prepare for a return to the field (against the Western Force). He told media:

> 'I'd had concussions before, and a week or so later you're back to feeling normal. In that respect [the latest concussion] was a lot different. Within that there's different feelings that play on your mind around anxiousness, which can certainly play with your head. All those things together can make it pretty tough ... The concussion and things with the head frustrate you but to get out of it you've got to work your way through those frustrations. Certainly, early on it was tough. Once I got a bit clearer about exactly what was going on with the body and head, it made things a bit easier and gave me a bit of time to reflect. It is scary when three or four weeks down the track you're still not feeling like you normally do. It's something that's pretty tough to handle; tough on the people around you because you're not yourself. You learn a lot going through it. Over the last couple of years it's increased the amount we're talking about it, which is a good thing. You want everyone to know how

> bad it can be and you've got to do the right thing by every individual that goes through it. I'm certainly more aware now that when something does happen to someone you make sure they're doing the right thing and not just trying to rush back onto the field. It made me realise exactly why we do this and how you feel when you are healthy ... feeling how you want to be you appreciate feeling great every day when you wake up.'

While Read looked to be his usual self in the Crusaders' 30–9 win over the Western Force, at the start of the following week he was not feeling well. Partly this was due to a head cold but post-concussion symptoms were being felt again.

As soon as word reached Steve Hansen of Read's condition he withdrew him from his All Blacks team to play England at Eden Park. Hansen told reporters:

> 'We're not prepared to risk him playing and that's our decision, not his, and we'll progress that day by day. Long term I'm not too concerned, but we're just not prepared risk him this week. He's frustrated, as you would be.'

While the English media seemed to be the only ones openly reacting with some delight that the player who had been in unstoppable form the last time the two sides met would not be appearing, Hansen added:

> 'Losing players is only disruptive if we allow it to be. Rugby is a contact sport; we're going to have people get injured and we just have to deal with that.'

Read sat out the first two tests, which were scrappy, patchy encounters won by the All Blacks 20–15 and 28–27, before being returned to the line-up for the final match in Hamilton. One reason for the added delay in his return was the caution on behalf of the All Blacks management team, who could see that Read was close to his old self on the training paddock but would benefit from one more match-free weekend.

He later told Sam Peters, a reporter for England's *Daily Mail* newspaper, that:

> 'Even though I wasn't showing any symptoms, obviously the brain wasn't quite right. You just get unlucky sometimes. It puts things in perspective when you have to take that time off. It makes you realise why you love playing this game and why I love being part of this team. I missed a couple of tests and it's not very nice when you have to watch the boys run out and you're not part of it.'

The Hamilton test was impressively won by the All Blacks, 36–13. It meant they had equalled the record for consecutive test wins by a top-tier international side. Read only played the first half in which the All Blacks stunned the visitors, scoring 29 points in the first half-hour. Savea had scored two tries before 10 minutes had passed!

In a cover story for *NZ Rugby World* magazine, Read told editor Gregor Paul:

> 'I look at the role of number eight as being pretty important in the overall context of the team. You have to be able to measure up physically, to stand up and compete with some fairly brutal and physical forward packs. And yet you also have to be able to provide a link with the backs — to almost play as another centre, I suppose. I love that you have to bring a whole different set of skills to the game, and I guess my key strength would be getting out there and running with the ball in hand.'

He was also aware of what being crowned the best player in the world would mean each time he stepped onto the field.

> 'I know that a lot of people will be coming at me, but that's pretty much how it is anyway. You can't really control that or worry about it — it happens every week that people want to measure themselves against you.'

When Super Rugby resumed after the Steinlager Series, the Crusaders finished second on points to the Waratahs, giving them a home semifinal against the Sharks. This they comprehensively won 38–6. They were off to Sydney to meet the Sydneysiders who had beaten the Brumbies 28–6 in their semi, but hadn't beaten the Crusaders in their 11 previous games since 2004.

As part of the promotional activities prior to Super Rugby finals, SANZAR has both captains meet at the ground wearing their team jerseys on the day before the match and to be photographed together with the trophy. The only problem this time was that the Waratahs' young skateboarding skipper Michael Hooper was nowhere to be seen at the appointed time. After 20 minutes of waiting Read left, only for Hooper to casually turn up some minutes later.

Adding fuel to the build-up fire was a comment about McCaw by Waratahs coach Michael Cheika, who was quoted in Sydney's *Daily Telegraph* newspaper:

'He's a really solid player; he never gives in; he's always there at the coalface of the battle; he's the type of player I like. Tomorrow we're not going to like him, obviously, we're going to try and go out there and hurt him.'

In the *Sydney Morning Herald*, rugby writer Paul Cully pointed to Read as the man the Waratahs had to focus on:

'The biggest threat to the Waratahs' Super Rugby finals chances is not the massive winger Nemani Nadolo, it is the man who has a licence to pop up on either wing, All Blacks number eight Kieran Read. The Crusaders have settled into a dangerous rhythm late in the season, and their hard work to get their back-rowers out wide is bearing fruit. The Crusaders have been cautious with Read after concussion-related spells out of the game this season, but last week all the familiar traits that made him the best player in the world last year re-emerged: the galloping stride, the offload, the power. There are a few players in each side capable of owning the final: Read is clearly one of them … Stop Read, and the Waratahs are halfway there.'

Read told media with what turned out to be some prescience that:

'It's important we stay focused and defend for long periods of time if we have to.'

The Waratahs began frenetically and in front of over 60,000 fans had raced to a 14–0 lead. Things

did not improve for the Crusaders when Carter limped off with what was later diagnosed as a break in his lower left leg. His departure from play was a repeat of his poor luck during the 2010 final against the Reds. Colin Slade replaced him and his kicking, as well as tries to Matt Todd and Nemani Nadolo, brought them back to parity with the New South Welshman. Then, with four minutes to go, Slade kicked a penalty to put the Crusaders out to a 32–30 lead. All the Cantabrians had to do was control the ball, and territory, for the final few minutes.

Instead halfback Willy Heinz anxiously opted to kick it away. Into touch. On the full. This gave possession back to the 'Tahs. With only seconds left to play, they had the ball at a ruck, midfield, and 10 metres into Crusaders territory. The ball appeared at the back of the ruck. McCaw swooped. Referee Joubert whistled and ruled rather contentiously that McCaw had infringed.

Penalty to the Waratahs.

Bernard Foley stepped up and kicked the winning goal. The Waratahs had their first Super Rugby title, 33–32.

In the emotion of the after-match period, a clearly disappointed Read told reporters:

'We didn't come here for this result, but you have to give full credit to New South Wales. When you give them the lead that we did it's very hard to run down. We probably didn't handle that pressure early on and let them get a roll on, and it was a case for us to get our hands on the ball and [create] our own pressure. In the second half we probably controlled it, and they had that one opportunity and they took it.'

McCaw, as always, was diplomatic about Joubert's penalising of him:

'I guess when you roll the dice that is what can happen. It's pretty gutting, really. Yeah … fifty-fifty, but in those moments, I probably should have known better really.'

On arriving back in Christchurch, coach Todd Blackadder told 3 News that 'to lose the game by, I'd say, a pretty dodgy call is really disappointing, but I'm proud of the way we fought back this season and I'm proud of the boys.' That 'dodgy call' was later the subject of a phone call from Joubert to Todd Blackadder, apologising for making the wrong decision.

When the 2014 Rugby Championship began, once again the All Blacks were on the verge of a world-record 18 consecutive test wins, but, just like in 2012, their opponents were the Wallabies and another disappointing draw brought their run to an end.

Conditions at the Olympic Stadium in Sydney were miserable, with rain falling throughout the game making the surface and the ball slippery throughout. The crowd of nearly 69,000 saw the Wallabies come back from 3–9 down at half-time and then level at 12–12 with All Black Beauden Barrett in the sin bin. (Wyatt Crockett also spent 10 minutes on the side-line naughty chair during the game.) Great defence saved the game for the All Blacks on a night when Wallaby captain Michael Hooper chose to kick for lineouts rather than points, and referee Jaco Peyper gave another of his puzzling displays as the man in charge.

For a team that had proved itself able to absorb or ignore pressure since 2011, securing their 18th test win had become the new bogeyman. McCaw told media after the game that there was:

'Certainly, a bit of a hollow feeling … you come to win and it didn't happen

… One thing is we get to have another crack next week so we'll keep the edge on at training.'

Hansen added:

'There's been a lot of talk about the world record, but the record comes about through winning games. So how do we feel about not winning games? Gutted.'

A week later, the two sides met again at Eden Park with the Wallabies again in search of their first win at the ground since 1986. The Wallabies had stopped the All Blacks setting a record for most consecutive test wins, then found themselves giving up a new record of their own — for most points conceded to the men in black — 51.

In what was labelled as a 'special performance' by Hansen, and a 'massacre' by some in the Australian media, the All Blacks completely dominated the Wallabies in every facet of the game.

McCaw had one of those games where he was justifiably sin-binned by referee Romain Poite, but also scored two tries.

Read scored a beauty himself, after a flying Savea grubber kicked infield from the wing, with the ball gathered 10 metres from the Australian line by replacement back Malakai Fekitoa. From a ruck on the line, Whitelock popped a short pass to Read, who crashed over by the posts. After the match, he commented:

'We needed our forward pack, especially the front five, to lay that platform. It was awesome … to win the Bledisloe and put fifty on is a massive effort.'

The win left the Wallabies without the Bledisloe Cup for the 12th season.

The 2014 Rugby Championship saw more titanic matches against South Africa and Australia. The first clash against the Springboks was on a blustery night in Wellington. The South Africans were at their most bruising with their eight-man, Duane Vermeulen, looking to knock flat anybody wearing a black jersey. The All Blacks dominated possession, but the bone-shuddering play of the Springboks forwards created pressure and thus mistakes at crucial times. The visitors led 7–6 at half-time.

Great Kieran Read All Blacks Moments #9

Test 67
New Zealand versus South Africa, 14–10
Westpac Stadium, Wellington
13 September 2014

Six minutes into the second half of the test against South Africa in Wellington, the Springboks led the All Blacks by one point, 7–6. The All Blacks were on attack. Aaron Smith passed back to Cruden from a ruck five metres from the Springboks' line. Cruden kicked across field to his right where Read was the only All Black. He jumped and caught the ball, five metres in from touch and five metres from the try line. Springbok captain Jean de Villiers wrapped up Read as he landed and tried to put him on the ground. But Read showed immense strength to stand in the tackle for several seconds (with his back to the try line) and — as Bryan Habana came in to help de Villiers — long enough to offload the ball to McCaw, who ran behind Read and around to score right in the corner.

Then, in a game of brute physicality, came that moment of incredible strength and subtlety from Read. The All Blacks won 14–10.

Stuff's rugby writers Toby Robson and Liam Napier rated Read 8.5 out of 10:

'Close to the best player on the park. Made four telling offloads — one to set up McCaw, and another which Aaron Smith spilled over the line. Topped the All Blacks' lineout takes with five, and made fourteen carries, the most from any forward. Seems to be nearing last year's form.'

After a win over Argentina against the Pumas (34–13), the All Blacks made their way to Ellis Park in Johannesburg where a raucous crowd of over 61,000 saw their side prevail 27–25.

Things didn't get any easier when the All Blacks met the Australians in Brisbane for their last match of the 2014 Rugby Championship. The Wallabies, who were getting more media coverage for coach Ewen McKenzie's off-field issues, were seen by some as being a shambles and ripe for an All Black hiding, as the men in black looked to bounce back after their South African loss. As so often seems to happen, things occurred very differently on the field.

The Wallabies put the All Blacks under pressure for (almost) 80 minutes and played some great rugby. The responses from the All Blacks, such as a quick tap for a try by Aaron Smith and a quick score for Cory Jane after a restart — the final pass coming from Read after one of his trademark surging runs — were superb, but errors broke their momentum … but not their spirit.

The final hooter sounded and they were down 28–22. Referee Craig Joubert played injury time in which the All Blacks mounted a final desperate attack inside the Wallabies' 22. Malakai Fekitoa, playing at 12, broke through the tackle of Bernard Foley and scored. But the All Blacks were still down 27–28. Colin Slade, who had replaced Beauden Barrett, had to make the side-line conversion for the win.

His kick never looked like missing. All Blacks 29, Australia 28.

Immediately after the match, McKenzie resigned as coach of the Wallabies. When Slade and Read then fronted the media, Read asked, 'What's the point of us being here?' with reference to the fact that the sensational departure of McKenzie would be the major sporting headline in the papers the next day.

The opening match of the All Blacks' 2014 northern tour was against the United States Eagles at the famous NFL ground, Soldier Field, in Chicago. A crowd of 61,500 — the largest to attend a rugby match in the United States — saw Read lead the All Blacks onto the field for the first time in over a year.

Build-up to the game had been somewhat festive as the All Blacks spent the week meeting sponsors and interacting with members of the public, as well as attending top US sporting fixtures in other codes, such as basketball and ice hockey.

The afternoon match saw an icy chill in the air, but both teams were quick to rev up as the Eagles forwards thrived on the early physical exchanges and the All Blacks threw the ball around from deep within their half. The condition of the field itself wasn't ideal, with the turf being easily dug up by scrums, but this didn't seem to affect big, bearded prop Charlie Faumuina, who delighted in running with ball in hand. Read scored one of the tries, and at the after-match press conference he congratulated the Eagles on the passionate way they had played. Despite the 74–6 score-line, they had retained the ball for long periods but struggled to make ground against the well-drilled and secure All Black defence.

In the lead-up to the next match, against England at Twickenham, the *Express* newspaper interviewed legendary All Black number eight Zinzan Brooke about his thoughts on Read. Brooke was most effusive:

'Sometimes you can have purple patches as a player, but Kieran Read has been consistently brilliant for the past three years. Kieran has been outstanding — in his offloading, his tackling, he's great at the tail of the lineout, solid at the scrum and does a fair bit of work in the loose. But more than anything, he's just so comfortable with the ball in hand. He isn't frightened to take on the defensive lines. Kieran makes offloading look so easy; it's what sets him apart. He's a miracle man. When you see it all the time as a fan, you can get a bit complacent — "Ah, Kieran Read has just done another one of those offloads." But it is so difficult to do that. And it's not just a one-off, he has done it against the best teams and the best defences on a consistent basis. When questions are asked of him, he delivers.'

It was high praise indeed from a man who had played 58 tests (1987–97) and whose on-field skills were often described as 'freakish', such was his ability to switch from playing as a traditional loose forward to an adventurous drop-kicker. His ball-handling skills were such that there were probably many basketballers who envied him! Read had grown up admiring the man they called 'Zinny', so was humbled by his praise.

The game against England was a strange one. The All Blacks won 24–21, with a last-minute penalty try awarded to England perhaps flattering the hosts who led on the scoreboard early but were outclassed for much of the second half. Most of the post-match attention focused on referee Nigel Owens, who had seemed swayed by the crowd at times and either overly relied on, or ignored, the Third Match Official (TMO).

The final match of the All Blacks' 2014 test campaign was against Wales in Cardiff. After the frustrating loss against England to end the 2012 season, and the nail-biting escape versus Ireland in 2013, the All Blacks wanted to finish the year on a high by not just winning, but winning in style.

Besides not wanting to spend the summer months away from rugby pondering another defeat, they had extra motivation to do well. McCaw was celebrating his 100th test as captain! No player in the history of the game had led his side in so many games. Ireland's tenacious and gifted centre Brian O'Driscoll had clocked up 84 matches as captain, and South Africa's hooking tyro, John Smit, had led his country 83 times. There was also another milestone to be celebrated if Keven Mealamu made it onto the field from the reserves bench: he would be making his 362nd appearance in a first-class match, and breaking the record held by the legendary Colin 'Pinetree' Meads, the man named as The All Black of the 20th Century. Meads had retired in 1971, 28 years before Mealamu first played for the Auckland team.

Wales had reason to give the match its all, too. They had not beaten the All Blacks since 1953 and their Kiwi coach Warren Gatland thought that this match would be their best chance in a long time to knock over the All Blacks. The Welsh players were so focused on the game, they'd barely scraped home the

week before against Fiji, having done them the disservice of considering them a walkover. The Red Dragons had narrowly escaped with a win of 17–13.

Come the All Black match, the Welsh team did all it could to stop the visitors playing at pace. The ball was slowed down at the breakdown and players in red jerseys seemed to require medical assistance — and even drinks of water — at every stoppage of play. With less than quarter of an hour to play, Wales were in front, 16–15. Then in a stunning final surge, the All Blacks scored three tries, two to replacement Beauden Barrett, and one to Read. In what seemed like the blink of an eye, the All Blacks had gone from one point down to winning by 18: 34–16. Welsh fans could not believe what had happened. All Blacks fans nodded sagely.

The half-time score of 3–3 seemed as though it had come from a completely different match.

The try Read scored was reward for his play in the match. While much of the focus had been on the master of the breakdown, Richie McCaw, it was actually Read who won the most turnovers for the team with four.

So the All Blacks finished the 2014 test season with a record of 12 wins, 1 loss and 1 draw (identical to that of 2012).

At the end of 2014, Steve Hansen's record as coach of the All Blacks stood at a staggering 90.4 per cent winning ratio — played 42, won 38, lost 2, drawn 2. As he said upon having his contract extended at the end of 2013:

'Our focus, as always, will be on enhancing the All Blacks' legacy. In doing that, it will be about not only winning test matches today, but also making sure we have the experience and personnel to win test matches tomorrow and beyond.'

Great Kieran Read All Blacks Moments #10

Test 73
New Zealand versus Wales, 34–16
Cardiff, Wales
22 November 2014

The All Blacks were out to a six-point lead in their final test of 2014 against Wales, and though it was apparent to them that the Welsh were tiring, it wasn't a secure lead. The slightest mistake could swing the game back to the home side, through an intercept pass or the adjudication of the referee. They had to keep playing inside the Welsh half and keep the pressure on. They did the former thanks to a couple of fine kicks from Aaron Smith. Then, following a Welsh lineout just on their own 22, the Welsh halfback went to kick from the back of a ruck. There was nothing laborious about the time he took to pick up the ball and swing his right leg for the hooked kick over the ruck, but by the time the ball left his boot, Read —

who had a clear run at him due to the fact no Welsh players were standing wide of the ruck — stormed through with his arms outstretched to charge down the kick. The ball ricocheted back off his body, spiralling over the slippery grass towards the corner flag. Read carried on his run, no doubt wary of a Welsh player coming across to tackle him as he reached the spinning ball. He could also see that it was getting close to the touchline. He had to pick the ball up off the grass in one motion and dive for the line, without spilling the ball or putting any part of his body over the touchline. And that is what he did. He made a potentially difficult manoeuvre look easy, and his try finally broke the resolve of the Welsh who knew, with eight minutes to play, that the All Blacks had withstood their aggression and determination for much of the game and then unleashed their own unforgiving skills and tactics on a weary team.

Hansen told Total Rugby:

'The All Blacks are expected to win every game so you don't get the luxury of going World Cup to World Cup, and we wouldn't want it any other way. Our fans set very high expectations, then the players have got to come in, and the management crew has got to come in over the top of that with their own expectations even higher. As a result, you get a pretty consistent performance from the team over many, many years … The jersey won't stand up on its own. It needs people to fill it up and do the right thing.'

When an eye was cast to the 2015 season and the looming Rugby World Cup in England, Read told Gregor Paul for a piece in the *Herald on Sunday*:

'It is not just playing a game of rugby. There's so much at stake for what this team means to so many people. The buzz you get out of it every time is huge. For me, it's pretty easy to get up for it. We want to continually be up the top. You want to say this week is important because a game you could potentially lose is when those great teams don't. But, bigger picture, next year becomes really important in terms of the standing of this team.'

The Future

Eyes then turned towards the 2015 Rugby World Cup and the All Blacks' preparation to become the first team to win the prized William Webb Ellis Trophy back to back.

Away from the glare of that tournament, another big challenge faces the All Blacks: life without Richie McCaw when he finally decides to retire. To many, Read is his natural successor as he has deputised for Richie many times at Super Rugby and international level. He is very much a player who is comfortable to lead from the front, and aspects of his play inspire his teammates and astound his fans. There is no question about that.

Read wrote a short piece for the University of Canterbury website about being a leader in professional sport:

'As players, we have to perform and deliver everything we learned and trained for to get the results we want. I thrive on the role of playing my part to support, challenge and guide my teammates so we get over the line each time. It's a huge commitment each year and I'm indebted to my wife, Bridget, and family for letting me enjoy giving my best if I am selected for these

teams. We also put life in perspective and realise we are very lucky to be fit and healthy and pulling on a Crusaders or All Blacks jersey ... While I have been lucky enough to win a few games over the years, I've also learned how to cope with and grow from defeat. The burning feeling you suffer from a loss takes a long time to get over, and the more you feel that pain, the more you can switch that energy into deeper determination to bounce back and reverse the result for the next game. It is easier to get a response from a loss, but knowing how to evolve while being successful is a true mark of a great leader.'

At the beginning of March 2015, London's *Telegraph* newspaper compiled a list of who their rugby writers and commentators saw as the best 100 players in world rugby. Twenty-one of the names on the list were All Blacks. (In fact, the lowest-ranked All Black was prop Tony Woodcock at number 83. So one could say that of the top 80 players in world rugby, a quarter of them were All Blacks!)

Topping the list was, of course, Richie McCaw. Who was at number two? Kieran Read, the man ready to take on the mantle of All Blacks captain. Most hearteningly for those All Black fans who worry about life after world cups, the players ranked three and four on the list were Brodie Retallick (World Player of the Year in 2014) and Julian Savea. Both players are still in their early twenties with long futures ahead of them.

Read has often spoken of the impact that playing in teams alongside McCaw has had on his maturation as a rugby player and leader. He told the *Daily Mail*'s Sam Peters:

> *'I grew up playing alongside Richie for the Canterbury Crusaders and the All Blacks so it wasn't too hard for me to switch into that kind of mind-set when you train alongside him every week. I probably always had that work rate and mentality inside myself but once you start working and training alongside someone like Richie, you see the level he lives up to every week. I just want to keep on improving and keep on getting better. That drives me on every day.'*

Inspired by the life and writings of Nelson Mandela, Read has also expressed admiration for a player in a rival code, the Argentine footballing star and Barcelona striker, Lionel Messi. As he told Peters:

> *'To me, when I look at a great player it is the consistency that sets them apart. The greats are the ones who do it every week. If you look across sports, someone like Lionel Messi scores goals every week, no matter who he's playing against.'*

Read's position as captain-in-waiting has seen him repeatedly quizzed by journalists about his views on team leadership. He told Sam Peters:

> *'It is something I get a great kick out of, to lead a team, and you not only do a lot of work throughout the week but on the field it is really enjoyable too. I love great players and the Crusaders team so it's amazing. There is a big workload, but those are the things which come with the honour of captaincy. You want to be adding to the team so you have to do that stuff. You can't let it faze you, you have to be the one who shows the strong face for the team and do extra things which need to be done.'*

The man who takes the field now in trademark black wristbands and black-and-white strapping about his forehead and thighs told Gregor Paul:

> *'I know my spot and I would love to be leading this team. It would be a great honour but when you have the best player in the world — the best All Black ever, the best captain ever — what it comes down to is me doing my bit for the team. We both love playing and leading to our best level and, generally, if we do, we are giving the chance for the All Blacks to win. I love being captain and I get a good kick out of it. There's extra motivation, I think, if you are captain. But hopefully that doesn't change my game too much.'*

All Black teams have not always had succession plans when it comes to captaincy, but (all going to plan) the team will become Read's to lead and he will do so with dedication, drive and the commitment to excel. Let's not forget that during the All Blacks' unbeaten season in 2013, he captained the side in six of the 13 matches. He will lead from the front and be the embodiment of the team on the great days, the average days, and the (hopefully few) bad days.

But Read has a life outside rugby, of course, and will also have a life *after* rugby, and is keen to instil in his daughters the importance of a good education. Studying for a qualification has been important to him and a routine part of his globetrotting, thanks to support from the University of Canterbury. In a University of Canterbury newsletter, Read's superviser, Glen Fyall, from the School of Sport and Physical Education, spoke of how the university has made it easier for students to continue studying while engaged in other activities, rather than seeing them drop out of tertiary education altogether:

> 'In recent years we have implemented flexible on-line learning that enables students like Kieran to achieve the qualification from anywhere in the world. I have worked with Kieran to see what suits his needs and allows him to continue to complete his sport coaching degree. We have worked with Kieran using our online course website, phone conversations, emails and texts. Many of the distance courses have videoed lectures that students can view wherever and whenever they want. With a busy family life, rugby and travel, Kieran suggests that his hotel room and the 'down time' when travelling are times that he can devote to study. Kieran's response, given his hectic

> schedule, has been fantastic and he has recently navigated his way through a course in sport coaching and leadership with a very good grade.'

Read has shown, from school visits in Christchurch as part of his studies through to coaching clinics in South America as part of his All Black commitments, that he has a genuine interest in young people developing an active interest in sport and physical education.

As something of a rarity for a professional sportsman, his form has rarely, if ever, been questioned. Opposing him over the past five years, the likes of Picamoles and Harinordoquy (France), Parisse (Italy), Spies and Vermeulen (South Africa), Heaslip (Ireland), Robert Jones and Faletau (Wales), Senatore (Argentina), Easter and Vunipola (England), McCalman and Higginbotham (Australia) have struggled for fitness, form, selection, or have through ill-discipline or through being in sides that have not been winning games, been less successful. None has made the impact on the international game over the same period in the way Read has. His career has not been sullied by off-field incidents or on-field spite. Text messages from his father before matches keep him grounded and focused. Sports fans, not just rugby fans, must hope that the rugby gods shine on the man who likes to relax listening to The Beatles, Coldplay and Kings of Leon, so that he remains free of concussion or other serious injury. If he does, the game of rugby will be better for it. The humble, quietly spoken supreme athlete of our game will cement his place as one of the giants of the game.

Appearances for New Zealand Age Group and Junior All Blacks Teams

2003

New Zealand Secondary Schools, in New Zealand and Australia

27 September	v **Samoa Schools**	at Wellington	74–13 (1 try)
1 October	v **Queensland Schools**	at Noosa	43–8
4 October	v **Australia Schools A**	at Southport	38–5 (replacement)
8 October	v **Australia Schools**	at Brisbane	18–16 (replacement)

2004

New Zealand Under 19 World Championships, South Africa

27 March	v **Ireland**	at Durban	30–6
31 March	v **Georgia**	at Durban	81–12 (2 tries, replacement)
4 April	v **Australia**	at Pietermaritzburg	30–5
8 April	v **South Africa**	at Durban (semifinal)	30–23
12 April	v **France**	at Durban (final)	34–11 (1 try)

2004

New Zealand Under 21 International Tournament, Argentina

9 June	v **Wales**	at Liceo RC, Mendoza	60–15 (replacement)
13 June	v **Canada**	at Mendoza RC	92–7
17 June	v **Australia**	at Chacras RC, Mendoza	43–46 (replacement)
21 June	v **South Africa**	at Liceo RC, Mendoza	12–16 (replacement)
25 June	v **France**	at Malvinas, Mendoza	47–21 (replacement)

2006

New Zealand Under 21 International Tournament, France

9	June	v **Italy**	at Riom	75–16 (replacement)
13	June	v **England**	at Vichy	29–14
17	June	v **Australia**	at Vichy	17–21
21	June	v **South Africa**	at Clermont-Ferrand (semifinal)	23–40
25	June	v **Australia**	at Clermont-Ferrand (3rd/4th play-off)	39–36 (subbed)

2007

Junior All Blacks, IRB Pacific Nations Cup

26	May	v **Samoa**	at Apia	31–10
9	June	v **Tonga**	at Nuku'alofa	39–13
23	June	v **Japan**	at Tokyo	51–3 (replacement)

Provincial and Super Rugby games

Canterbury (2006–2009) — 37 games, 50 points (10 tries)
Crusaders (2007–2015) — 119 games, 90 points (18 tries)

All Blacks Appearances to 31 December 2014

2008

8 November	v **Scotland**	at Edinburgh	32–6
15 November	v **Ireland**	at Dublin	22–3 (replacement 71 mins)
18 November	v **Munster**	at Limerick	18–16 (replacement 51 mins)
29 November	v **England**	at London	32–6 (replacement 55 mins)

2009

13 June	v **France**	at Dunedin	22–27
20 June	v **France**	at Wellington	14–10
27 June	v **Italy**	at Christchurch	27–6
18 July	v **Australia**	at Auckland	22–16 (replacement 61 mins)
25 July	v **South Africa**	at Bloemfontein	19–28 (replacement 53 mins)
1 August	v **South Africa**	at Durban	19–31 (replacement 60 mins)
22 August	v **Australia**	at Sydney	19–18
12 September	v **South Africa**	at Hamilton	29–32
19 September	v **Australia**	at Wellington	33–6
31 October	v **Australia**	at Tokyo	32–19 (replacement 53 mins)
7 November	v **Wales**	at Cardiff	19–12 (subbed 68 mins)
21 November	v **England**	at London	19–6
28 November	v **France**	at Marseille	39–12 (subbed 72 mins)

2010

12 June	v **Ireland**	at New Plymouth	66–28 (1 try)
19 June	v **Wales**	at Dunedin	42–9 (subbed 70 mins)
26 June	v **Wales**	at Hamilton	29–10 (subbed 63 mins)
10 July	v **South Africa**	at Auckland	32–12 (1 try)
17 July	v **South Africa**	at Wellington	31–17
31 July	v **Australia**	at Melbourne	49–28
7 August	v **Australia**	at Christchurch	20–10
21 August	v **South Africa**	at Johannesburg	29–22
11 September	v **Australia**	at Sydney	23–22 (1 try)
30 October	v **Australia**	at Hong Kong	24–26
6 November	v **England**	at London	26–16 (1 try)
13 November	v **Scotland**	at Edinburgh	49–3
20 November	v **Ireland**	at Dublin	38–18 (2 tries)
27 November	v **Wales**	at Cardiff	37–25 (subbed 35 mins)

2011

6 August	v **Australia**	at Auckland	30–14
27 August	v **Australia**	at Brisbane	20–25 (subbed 12 mins)
2 October	v **Canada**	at Wellington (RWC pool match)	79–15 (subbed 51 mins)
9 October	v **Argentina**	at Auckland (RWC quarterfinal)	33–10 (1 try)
16 October	v **Australia**	at Auckland (RWC semifinal)	20–6
23 October	v **France**	at Auckland (RWC final)	8–7

2012

9 June	v **Ireland**	at Auckland	42–10
16 June	v **Ireland**	at Christchurch	22–19 (subbed half-time)
18 August	v **Australia**	at Sydney	27–19
25 August	v **Australia**	at Auckland	22–0
8 September	v **Argentina**	at Wellington	21–5
15 September	v **South Africa**	at Dunedin	21–11
29 September	v **Argentina**	at La Plata	54–15
6 October	v **South Africa**	at Johannesburg	32–16
20 October	v **Australia**	at Brisbane	18–18
17 November	v **Italy**	at Rome	42–10 (captain, 1 try)
24 November	v **Wales**	at Cardiff	33–10
1 December	v **England**	at London	21–38 (1 try)

2013

8 June	v **France**	at Auckland	23–13 (captain)
15 June	v **France**	at Christchurch	30–0 (captain)
22 June	v **France**	at New Plymouth	24–9 (captain)
17 August	v **Australia**	at Sydney	47–29
24 August	v **Australia**	at Wellington	27–16
7 September	v **Argentina**	at Hamilton	28–13
14 September	v **South Africa**	at Auckland	29–15 (captain, 2 tries)
28 September	v **Argentina**	at La Plata	33–15 (captain)
5 October	v **South Africa**	at Johannesburg	38–27 (1 try)
19 October	v **Australia**	at Dunedin	41–33 (captain, 1 try)
9 November	v **France**	at Paris	26–19 (1 try)
16 November	v **England**	at London	30–22 (1 try)
24 November	v **Ireland**	at Dublin	24–22

2014

21 June	v **England**	at Hamilton	36–13 (subbed half-time)
16 August	v **Australia**	at Sydney	12–12
23 August	v **Australia**	at Auckland	51–20 (1 try)
6 September	v **Argentina**	at Napier	28–9
13 September	v **South Africa**	at Wellington	14–10
27 September	v **Argentina**	at La Plata	34–13
4 October	v **South Africa**	at Johannesburg	25–27
18 October	v **Australia**	at Brisbane	29–28
1 November	v **USA**	at Chicago	74–6 (captain, subbed 54 mins)
8 November	v **England**	at London	24–21
22 November	v **Wales**	at Cardiff	34–16 (1 try)

Played 73 (72 tests): Won 63, Lost 8, Drawn 2
Captained: 8
Test tries: 17

Acknowledgements

I must acknowledge the partnership between the New Zealand Rugby Museum and allblacks.com, which provides an easily accessible and up-to-date online record of All Blacks rugby (to refresh the memory in the era of a multitude of test matches each year). Similarly, the annual *Rugby Almanack of New Zealand* is indispensable. My thanks to the rugby scribes named within for their great coverage of our game.

Thanks to Bill Honeybone (Publisher at David Bateman Ltd) for asking me to write about a player whose skills I delight in watching, whose attitude is highly laudable, and who has become a hero to so many All Blacks fans, both young and old. Thanks also to Antoinette Sturny, Eva Chan and Cheryl Smith.

Special thanks to my wife, Mel, son, Peter, and Murray (for his ongoing interest).

About the Author

Among a number of titles, Matt is the author of the bestselling biography of Billy T. James, *Billy T: The Life and Times of Billy T James* (reviewed in *North & South* magazine as 'the biography of the year'). He chronicled the life of 1905 All Black captain and soldier, Dave Gallaher, in 2012, *Dave Gallaher: The Original All Black Captain*. His collaboration with cartoonist Chris Slane — *Nice Day for a War: Adventures of a Kiwi Soldier in WWI* — was based on Elliott's grandfather's Western Front diaries, and won the Book of the Year and the Non-fiction prizes at the 2012 New Zealand Post Children's Book Awards.

Matt has lived in Melbourne, Christchurch, Ireland and Wellington, but now resides back in his home town of Auckland, with his wife and young son.

mattelliottnz.com